# Great Preaching
# Today

# Great Preaching Today

*Edited by Alton M. Motter*

A COLLECTION OF 25 SERMONS
DELIVERED AT THE CHICAGO SUNDAY
EVENING CLUB

HARPER & BROTHERS PUBLISHERS NEW YORK

*Dedicated to*

*JOHN NUVEEN*

*Who—since the death in 1944 of the first president and founder, Clifford W. Barnes—has served as the second president of the Chicago Sunday Evening Club*

# Contents

# Acknowledgments

Special acknowledgment is made to those contributors whose manuscripts appeared earlier, either in exact or modified form, in the following publications, and to the publishers who have also granted permission for inclusion in this volume:

Ralph J. Bunche, the *Christian Century* (April, 1953); Henry Hitt Crane, *Those Prophetic Voices,* Whitmore and Stone (1942); J. Wallace Hamilton, *Horns and Halos in Human Nature,* Fleming H. Revell (1954); James A. Pike, *Beyond Anxiety,* Charles Scribner's Sons (1953); Liston Pope, *Saturday Review of Literature* (September, 1952) and subsequently in Bantam Book, *Saturday Review Reader No. 2;* and Paul M. Robinson, *The Pulpit* (June, 1951).

# Preface

Do today's outstanding Christian leaders have a message for our time? If so, do they deserve a wider hearing? This collection of twenty-five sermons delivered before the Chicago Sunday Evening Club answers the first question. The second question is answered by the thousands of people in the Sunday Evening Club's wide radio audience who request these messages by mail.

A first volume containing fifteen such messages was published in 1952 by Harper & Brothers under the title, *Sunday Evening Sermons*. The foreword to that volume also contains a brief historical background of the Chicago Sunday Evening Club which should be of interest to those who are not acquainted with this unique organization in American religious life.

This second and larger volume of addresses and sermons is published with the belief that additional thousands of people will welcome the opportunity of joining an increasingly wider reading audience. Geographically the twenty-five contributors, with one exception, come from every section of the United States. Denominationally, they come from nine church bodies. Three are laymen. The volume contains, therefore, a cross-section of contemporary American preaching.

The content of the volume is equally varied. Over one-fourth of the sermons deal with the development of a more meaningful and personal relationship with God. Another fourth express a vital concern for man's social responsibility toward his fellow man. A few sermons deal with distinctly theological themes. A number of others emphasize the role of religion in political and international life.

9

For the most part, here is preaching which attempts to speak to our deep spiritual hungers. To the extent that this is achieved it is *great* preaching. We dare to hope that our readers will agree with this evaulation as they find these messages meeting the religious needs of their own hearts and minds.

Some time ago, a member of the audience was asked why he attended the Chicago Sunday Evening Club, now going into its forty-eighth year. He replied, "In order to have my spiritual batteries recharged." This volume is offered with the hope that it may be the means by which many others may have such an experience.

ALTON M. MOTTER

*January, 1955*
*Orchestra Hall, Chicago*

# Great Preaching
# Today

# 1

## Toward Peace and Freedom

### By RALPH J. BUNCHE

IN THE INTERNATIONAL COMMUNITY, THE UNITED NATIONS, among whose servants I am proud to be numbered, seeks morality and brotherhood as the basis of human relations. For the United Nations knows that in no community—local, national or international—can there be security, progress and hope unless the conduct of its members is governed by moral law and a minimum spirit of fellowship. The United Nations, in its short seven years of existence in this turbulent postwar period, has made only a beginning; indeed, a feeble beginning in many respects. But who can be so blind, so narrow, so indifferent to moral values and world needs as to suggest that the effort should never have been made or should now be abandoned?

I am acutely conscious that in some quarters there is opposition—as bitter as it is blind and unreasoning—to the United Nations. This hostility has intensified in some areas, despite the fact that support for the U.N. and its principles is a fundamental policy of our new national administration, as it was of the former administration. But I am fully confident that the generality of

*Ralph J. Bunche, former director of the United Nations, department of trusteeship, is now Under-Secretary without portfolio for the U.N.*

people in our country believe in the kind of international order the United Nations seeks to create. They long for security, for peace and for freedom. They wish to see the U.N. succeed. If they are critical of it—and they have good reason to be critical—this is no manifestation of opposition to its objectives, but an understandable expression of disappointment and disillusionment that it has not done more and served better the hopes of all of us. I certainly share this disappointment, but I do not let it blind me to the successes the United Nations has had—and they have been many—to the great services it has rendered, and to the potentiality it has, given understanding support, for far greater service to humanity in the future.

Now, people in society can live together only if their relations are governed by some recognition, however imperfect, of moral law and mutual respect. The nations of the world, which make up the international community, must be similarly governed in their relationships or there will be international chaos on a scale beggaring description and with consequences, in this atomic era, too forbidding to contemplate. In our society, in every society, there are rebels, mavericks and evildoers who refuse to govern their conduct by any accepted code. But we do not abandon the effort to create and maintain and perfect the society because of them. To the contrary, it is precisely because of them that laws, police and moral pressures are indispensable to our existence.

The analogy to the international community has even greater compelling force. It is only through strong moral pressure, through laws and police (which in international affairs take the form of collective security) that any nation can find protection against maverick nations and the forces of evil now loose in the world.

Ideals are goals toward which all men and women of good will strive. We know all too well, of course, that in the realm of practical affairs our ideals are never fully achieved. But we do not take our eyes from them and cease to strive, simply because the path is arduous and the obstacles formidable. If we did so we would abandon all religion, all morality, and prepare to return to the jungle.

If we would not think of following such a defeatist and disastrous course in our community affairs, why should we do so in the international community, where both the need and the danger are far greater? I assure you that despite all obstacles, all frustrations and setbacks, the United Nations will persist steadfastly in its effort to build an international community in which moral law shall prevail.

It is only as sincere effort is exerted to realize them that ideals assume practical meaning. Peace and freedom are high on the list of our American ideals, as they are the basic ideals of the United Nations. We in America are devoted to these ideals. Our future and, indeed, the future of civilization depends upon their preservation.

Here we are confronted with the dilemma of our times. How is peace to be achieved and preserved in a world in which the so-called "cold war" is being waged ever more intensively and universally; in which a tragic, frustrating, costly and bitterly fought "localized war" in Korea has been prolonged for nearly three years; in which all of us live fearfully in the shadow of the ever-present threat of atomic war? And how is the ideal of freedom to be preserved and extended in a world in which many peoples, having once enjoyed freedom, have now lost it to totalitarianism; in which, in truth, relatively few—far too few—people have ever enjoyed it at all; and in which it is everywhere menaced today?

Now we in America cannot escape the fact that the future of the ideals of peace and freedom will depend in very large measure on us, on America and Americans—on our policies, our wisdom, our sincerity; on our courage, patience and tenacity; on our ability to understand and to win and hold the confidence of other peoples, of different colors, cultures, races and nationalities throughout the world who also cherish peace and freedom.

What course are we in America to follow? The decisions we are called on to make are momentous, for no less than the future of all civilization hinges on them. How and by what road, if not the United Nations, are we to seek peace and freedom and justice in the world?

As I listen to the hue and cry of the critics of the U.N. these days, I listen intently, and in vain, to learn what alternative they may have to offer. It is much easier to turn off a known road than to locate a new one. I find the constructive record of the critics utterly barren.

For example, think of the crescendo of criticism about the tragedy of Korea. Most of us know that, tragic and painful as it has been, it was right for the United Nations and the United States to oppose aggression in Korea; that it would have been a shameful and fateful, if not fatal, weakness to abandon the Republic of Korea to the Communist aggressors from the north. If the United Nations had not intervened, in all probability American boys would be fighting elsewhere today and in a far greater war. And having intervened with the sole purpose of protecting South Korea, could sanity advise us to take responsibility before the bar of world opinion for expanding the Korean war into the dreaded world atomic war?

We must, it seems to me, ponder honestly the question whether, despite the obvious weaknesses of the United Nations and all the disillusionment about it, there is really any sensible and practical alternative to it. That is the question.

There have been United Nations failures, of course. But where have there been greater successes? May we not ask ourselves whether we, as Americans, who have so very much at stake, have done all we could do to make the United Nations a better, stronger and more effective force in world affairs? What critic of the United Nations has come forth with a more promising way? There are answers, of a sort. But it seems to me that the answers are essentially escapist.

World government, with an idealism which reaches for the international millennium, is one such. But in view of the harsh realities of international life today and the strong current of nationalism among all the peoples of the world, this must today be regarded as at worst a misleading slogan and at best a romantic notion.

Neo-isolationism, the postwar version of our prewar outmoded aloofness from the affairs of the world, is another and more popular escapism. But I cannot for the life of me understand how anyone could seriously counsel an isolationist policy for our nation today. To pursue such a policy would be little short of suicidal. We are a very strong nation and people, and we are capable of even greater strength, but in this new age we cannot ever again be safe alone in the world. Of that fact I am sure.

In this regard, let us not forget that the objective of both sides engaged in the cold war is to win people, to win friends, to win adherents. It must be clear therefore that in a world-wide struggle, thus far more ideological than military, whose stakes are no less than the minds and hearts of the peoples of the world, isolationism is a vehicle as antiquated as the one-horse shay. We must have guns, of course, but in this world friends, tried and true friends who believe as we do, are as imperative as armaments.

Moreover, without an international organization such as the United Nations, how is the effort to be made to settle peacefully the multitude of differences which endanger the world? These include not only the major conflict between West and East, between democracy and communism, but many, many more. Indeed many of them, even posing threats to peace, have no direct relationship whatsoever to the democracy-communist conflict. Surely we cannot have reached that depth of despair or impatience wherein we are prepared to abandon all effort to resolve international disputes peacefully and to rely exclusively on the arbitrament of war. Patience is one of the most powerful weapons in this titanic world struggle, and let us never forget it.

It is the United Nations alone which is designed and equipped to seek peaceful resolution of differences among nations. Within the framework of the United Nations, consultations and negotiations on all the vital problems of the international community are constantly under way. In and out of the meetings, the discussions—formal and informal, individual and collective—go on. The range of interest is staggering. To the meetings of the General Assembly come regularly the foreign ministers of the five great powers and many smaller nations. How could they all be brought together for extensive periods each year except through the United Nations? They debate, they consult with each other, and they frequently indulge in propaganda speeches designed more for external than United Nations consumption. There is endless talk, there is acrimony and anger, but there is also often agreement. But in any case, who would question that the babble of many tongues in heated, even angry debate, is a heartening substitute for the deadly thunder of war? Better always to argue than to shoot.

These representatives of the sixty member nations of the United Nations are all, Eastern and Western alike, constantly exposed to the pressure of world opinion, and in varying degree they are highly sensitive to it and influenced by it even while striving to influence and win it.

If impasses can possibly be broken, if peaceful solutions or approaches to solutions of the pressing problems of the world can be found, how can this be better done? Surely not by a formal division of the world into bristling armed camps. And certainly not through the rigid, stilted formalities of classical diplomatic intercourse. Without the United Nations, every problem, every incident, indeed, in these times of tension, almost every diplomatic note, would be a potential provocation to war. United Nations experience has demonstrated that the harsh words of angry debate lose much of their sting in the social intercourse after the meetings. Moreover, strong language, often repeated in public meetings, comes soon to be regarded as routine and is ignored, except perhaps by the shocked public in the galleries, many of whom come to be shocked.

We do well to reflect on the fact that the representatives of sixty nations come regularly, at no little expense to their taxpayers, from all over the world to the frequent meetings of the various organs of the United Nations. They come year after year, month after month—representatives of western Europe, of the British Commonwealth, of Asia, of Latin America, of the Middle East, and of the Soviet bloc, even though their positions and propositions are voted down almost invariably. Nations not in the organization seek to gain admission to it.

Why do they come if the organization is as futile as some of its critics paint it? There is little they can hope to take back to their countries to indulge selfish national desires. The United Nations serves international, not national, interests. These representatives come because their peoples demand that they come, for their peoples cherish hope and can find no nourishment for it other than in the United Nations. It is significant that no member nation of the U.N. has ever withdrawn from it, even though its actions on occasion have so displeased some members that they have stalked angrily out of its meetings—only to walk back in again later. In one notable instance they walked back in seven months later. But they walked back.

The United Nations has achieved an effective international community, a family of nations, in embryo, with international public opinion as an increasingly strong sanction. There would be much to lose and little to gain for any nation deciding to leave the United Nations and stand alone. So we are not discouraged, never discouraged, no matter how grave the setbacks, for we dare not permit ourselves to become discouraged. We know that the price of United Nations failure is world-wide atomic war, and from this unspeakable catastrophe we remain resolutely determined to save mankind. We will not ignore, deride or scoff at any gesture, any hint from any source that may offer the slightest hope of progress for an honorable peace.

We are realists in the United Nations, and we know that one of its vital functions is to serve as a lightning rod in the arena of international politics. It may often be the case that the United Nations can lessen the dangerous tension and serve the interests of peace by taking unmerited blows and acting as scapegoat, and in this role we have increasing experience.

Some of the letters I receive are critical of the United Nations, and in some instances literally scorch the paper on which they are written. There is a simple pattern to these denunciatory missives: the writers declare that the United Nations is no good and they praise America. I also praise America, for this is a very good and a very great country. But this isn't the issue at all. The issue is: How is America, strong and good as it is, going to preserve its own freedom without contributing its full share to the peace and freedom of the world?

It seems to me only elemental common sense to say that one just does not jump off a life raft into a stormy sea because the life raft, even though still afloat, isn't much of a boat, or, forsooth, because it isn't painted red, white and blue. The United Nations is the world's life raft today. Granted that we would all prefer a sturdier and more seaworthy craft, we should be very thankful that we have this raft.

Soon after my return from Palestine, I spoke in support of the United Nations, which had just stopped another dangerous war in Palestine. My belief in it is no less ardent today. It is not really the United Nations as an organization to which I am devoted, but rather the ideals and principles and objectives to which it is committed. For how can civilization and mankind survive and progress unless we have peace, unless people everywhere are free, unless there is hope for progressively improving living standards for all people, unless there is morality and justice—international as well as national—unless racial and religious bigotry are eliminated and we can cultivate a true spirit of brotherhood among men? And how are we to serve these ends if we do not bring the nations and peoples of the world together, friend and foe alike? Is this not the Christian way? And is there any other way?

The principles of the United Nations are sound. They chart the only course to a free and peaceful world and an international moral order in our time. In international affairs, as in personal affairs, it is important that one have some faith, that one have an anchor in faith, and the United Nations in international affairs is mine. In my view, national self-interest and collective interest become broadly identical in the United Nations. As an American, devoted and loyal to my country and proud of my country, I endorse the United Nations if only because the international objectives it pursues serve well, very well indeed, the interests of my country and of all my fellow countrymen.

# 2

# The Search for God

## By GEORGE A. BUTTRICK

CHILDREN ASK "WHERE IS GOD?" WE ASK, FOR AS WE CON-
front the inscrutible mystery of life, we are always children.
When we measure ourselves against children, we know more than
they, and are inordinately proud of the knowledge; but when we
measure ourselves against the mystery, we know little more than
they, and are still children. So Gamaliel Bradford wrote:

> Gleaming bits of quaint desire tempt my
>   steps beyond the decent.
> I confound old solid glory with publicity
>   too recent.
> But my one unchanged obsession, wheresoe'er
>   my feet have trod,
> Is a keen, enormous, haunting, never-sated
>   thirst for God.[1]

He was asking the child's question—and the man's question.

*George A. Buttrick was the pastor of the Madison Avenue Pres-
byterian Church, New York City, for 28 years and has edited
the twelve-volume commentary, "The Interpreter's Bible." He
is now a member of the faculty of Harvard Divinity School.*

[1] "God," from *Shadow Verses* by Gamaliel Bradford. Used by permission
of Yale University Press.

This age is called "secular." I wonder! Perhaps it is secular only in the sense that we have quit looking for God; not because our thirst is stilled, but because, not having found God down any of our chosen paths, we have decided it is no use looking. But the word "God" is still on our lips, and it somehow comes naturally, as it does to a child. When we curse and swear we instinctively use the word "God": a curse needs something ultimate to ratify it. When a child is born, we exclaim, though our language may not be religious: "Surely God was in this place, and I knew it not!" When death comes, we know that we are in the hands of an irrevocable will, and exclaim: "Verily thou art a God that hidest thyself!"

Secular? Perhaps. At least we dimly see that the thing basically wrong with communism is that it tries to turn a group of men into God, that it has no throne in the heavens. We vaguely know that this orange of a world, if it is merely secular, is dry in pith and fruit, however golden its promise. The question may be muffled nowadays, but only in a numbness that may at any moment become an agony: "Oh that I knew where I might find him!"

Could it be that we have been looking for the wrong kind of God? Could it be? If you have been told that the stranger whom you are to meet at the depot will be wearing a blue suit, and that he will be hatless, bald-headed, with dark horn-rimmed glasses; and if he comes wearing rimless glasses, a homburg, a light gray suit, and tan shoes—you will miss him. Could it be that we look for the wrong kind of God? Job looked for a God who plainly in this world rewarded the righteous and punished the wicked. The religious community of that day told Job that God is always plainly in that character, and Job could not find the evidence—at least, not the clear evidence.

Perhaps the present-day church still gives that false description of God. Perhaps the church has helped to provoke communism.

Benjamin Jowett said to Margot Asquith: "My dear child, you must believe in God in spite of what the clergy tell you." There is no indisputable evidence on this planet, at least within the space of one man's lifetime, that God always rewards the righteous in strict proportion, and always thus punishes the wicked.

Suppose there were such a God! An accountant in the sky forever balancing the celestial ledgers! We need accountants, but not as God. For under such a God all goodness might become prudential shrewdness, and our whole world would be icebound. But Job thought he wanted that kind of God, because Job thought he had been unjustly treated: "I would order my cause before him, and fill my mouth with arguments." He thought God would arrive with account books and a pen in His ear, and a porter pushing his desk and files; and so Job missed God.

What kind of a God are you looking for? A God who will answer all your intellectual questions, lackey to your intellectual pride? A God who will solve all mysteries, a God who will go your pace, and be no larger than the measure of your understanding? In that case, you would be God; and—forgive me!—that would be a nightmare. Perhaps we are looking for the wrong kind of God. By the way, if God is always to deal with us in strict justice, what heaven would any of us deserve?

Perhaps we have been looking for God in the wrong place. If that stranger at the train arrived at platform three, and you waited at platform twenty-two, you would miss Him. Job said: "I will look for him on the outside of things, in the world. If the storm strikes the house of the good man and by-passes the house of the crook, I shall know there is no God." It is hardly too much to allege that for generations we have been looking for God in the scheme of things, and refusing any tests except scientific tests. Again, we need science, but not as a way of finding God. If God were a law or a thing, science might be the way to find Him. But if God is the unseen Companion (what other kind of God would be Godlike?), why should we expect to find Him in things? God's works presumably will give some hint of His nature: a tidal wave killing hundreds in Hawaii will tell us that He is not concerned very much with the treasuring of our flesh, and a sunset may make Tennyson exclaim to his friend Hallam, "What an imagination God has!" But even so, we can hardly expect to find the Artist by scrutinizing His canvas, or by dissecting the furniture He has made.

You and I: have we been searching a realm of things in the expectation of finding God? We still need science—in its place. But its place will shrink; that overemphasis will pass. To ransack the house will never introduce us to the owner, much less to grab whatever cash can be found. Even to read the letters on his desk will not make a friendship. If God is Person, Super-Person if you will, He will presumably be found in the realm of the personal. If He is Spirit, as all great seers have said, presumably we shall find Him in our spirit—perhaps even in our fierce protest against a Church that offers us conventional doctrines. "Oh that I knew where I might find him!" But suppose we have been waiting at the wrong platform!

*Let us speak bluntly: we ourselves by ourselves can never find God except as God finds us, or lets Himself be found.* If we use the word God, with some sense, however vague, of what the word means, we have already found God; or rather, been found of Him. Thus Pascal said (was he not right?) that he could not seek God had he not already found Him. Suppose the exclamation "Oh that I knew where I might find him!" is itself the gift of God. Take an extreme instance, the quatrain from the *Rubáiyát* by Omar Khayyám:

> O Thou, who man of baser earth didst make,
> And e'en with paradise devise the snake;
> For all the sin wherewith the face of man
> Is blackened—man's forgiveness give—and take!

It has the sound of blasphemy. But there is indignation in it, yes, and compassion for man's lot amid the "slings and arrows of outrageous fortune." Suppose God is in the indignation and the compassion. Is it fair to identify God with the seeming cruelty, and rule Him out from the pity? Yet that is what we do! Grant Him in the pity, the mystery remains, but it has chance to become a luminous mystery—like the first silver mist of the day-break.

So where is God? In the movement of your secret spirit. He is in the agonizing question "Where is God?" He is in the protest that a world of wars is a Godless world. He may not be found in the stars, at least not quickly, but He may be found in the impulse which makes a man study the stars; for that far-off real estate cannot be bought or sold, and any man who studies the stars has the touch of wonder on him, wonder being incipient worship. Carlyle looked at the stars, and exclaimed, "Man, it's terrible!" So it is, for there are terrors in God: He refuses to be cabined in our little complacencies and comforts.

But what of the astronomer who confronts the terrors, and finds a music of the spheres, and is vaster in heart still than any vastness he can discover? Surely God is in that man's spirit! Surely God is even closer to the life of a Eugene Debs exclaiming, "While there is a soul in prison I am not free!" Surely God is there, even though Debs may deny God. So let us say that God is in the movement of man's spirit. The doctor, dissecting a corpse, allowed that he could "find no soul." He could not have found any even if the man had been alive, at least not that way. But whence came the world "soul," and who prompted him to search?

Where then is God? In Jesus Christ. That faith is too stagger-ing in its fine avowal to be untrue. God is not the keeper of ledgers to punish any man in debt: He is in the debtor's prison in place of the debtor. God does not "devise the snake," or wantonly begrime mankind in this life's smoke: He shares with man the darkened road, and carries the heavy end of the burden. He is not an Egotist, His ME stamped on every sky and shouted on every wind: He is love coming into our world in great humility. How do we know? By Christ himself! There is no argument to prove God: He is His own evidence. A legend says of a statue on the Nile that music came from it at every new dawn to lift the hearts of all in that wide valley. The would-be conqueror smashed the statue thinking thus to break the spirit of the Nile people. But all in vain: the music still came from the ruins of the statue. Try to break Christ, call him only one more man making one more guess: his music is not silenced. He lifts the heart of every man in the valley called earth. Had any other died on his Cross it would have been still a gallows. He dies there—a man can partly carry his brother's burden, but only God can carry the weary load of mankind—he dies there, and the Cross becomes a shrine.

Where then is God? In the surrender of a man's will to Him. What else can a man do with God-in-Christ? The New Testament word is "believe." It is not at its core a theological word, though it gathers to itself a theology. It means "by your leave": it is the utter pledge of the soul. How else could we expect to find God? Even a human friendship requires a measure of surrender: each opens wide the door to the other's mind. Even human love is unfulfilled without a plighted troth "until death us do part."

God having given Himself in Jesus Christ, how can we know Him except in glad surrender? To treat Him as a weekend custom, or as one interest among many (which is the modern attitude), is to drive Him away in pain—like some renewed Calvary. Not even human friendship could endure on those terms! No, God being in Christ, a man loses God (in the shadow which man himself makes as he turns from light) when he rejects God's overture of love. As God in Christ has knelt to dress the wound of mankind, having sucked away the sting, so man (meaning you and me) must kneel before God: "Dear my Lord, I am liege man of Thine, for life and limb and earthly regard; and I will be true to Thee, come life, come death, so help me God!" Only so can we find Him! By any other response we drive Him from our door, though still He will wait and hope.

Job wanted an explanation of pain, or at least some vindication in the midst of tragedy. So do we: God must answer our questions, or we will declare that there is no God. Even so, Job was nearer God than the conventional religionists of that time who insisted that events always clearly punish the wicked and always clearly reward the righteous, for Job at least kept honesty—and God is truth. But God does not give any neat explanation of suffering, and there is no clear evidence (in the span of one man's lifetime and in every detail of life) that the wicked are always justly punished and the good always justly rewarded. God ought to be somewhat larger than an account book.

Besides, do we know what good fortune is, or evil fortune? Many a man has become gentle through suffering, and many another man has become crass through abundant health. Yes, the reverse can be true: a man may become sour through suffering, and his neighbor may become generous through his good health. But that leaves the issue where we stated it: Do we know what is blessing or catastrophe? The answer is in our response to life, in the realm of faith; yes, in the pledge of ourselves to the God whom we see in Jesus. For if God Himself shares the suffering, our question is answered far better than in a neat explanation.

"Oh that I knew where I might find him!" The cry has been on your lips. But why? That you might have your questions all answered? That you might exact your "rights" from God? If God is thus to be your servant, you would be God, not He! The woman said that God had required her to pray to Him thirty-six times a day, and she was afraid that she had failed. Her minister retorted: "To hell with that kind of God!" But maybe our kind of God is no better: an Accountant keeping exact ledgers. Where have you expected to find God? In the outer world? There is evidence of Him there, but you do not find even a human friend by analyzing his shoes or even by examining his skin. Perhaps your cry is itself the cry of God in you! Perhaps the final word comes from One who climbed a dark hill carrying a darker burden: "He that hath seen me hath seen the Father."

# 3

# Thermometers versus Thermostats

## By HENRY HITT CRANE

CONFRONTED WITH A WORLD IN CHAOS, WITH NATIONS ARRAYED against one another in deadly strife, with militant and conflicting ideologies bewildering and bulldozing everybody, the obvious problem of all contemporary problems is perhaps best summed up in the urgent query, What is it all about?

To get any kind of working hypothesis that is at all satisfactory, we must resort to generalizations, despite the quip that "all generalizations are false, including this one." And even at the risk of oversimplifying such a frightfully complex problem, we must choose some symbols to express the clarifying generalizations. Suppose, therefore, we adopt two fairly familiar modern symbols which we can set in contrast to each other as suggesting the two conflicting principles underlying the universal struggle.

Consider first the *thermometer*. Essentially, it is merely an instrument which reveals, records or registers its environments by unhesitatingly responding to it. Whatever the temperature, no matter how hot or how cold, the thermometer reflects it. The tiniest fluctuation in the external conditions is immediately recognized by the thermometer in its expansive or contractive reaction.

*Henry Hitt Crane is the pastor of the Central Methodist Church, Detroit.*

It conforms completely to the environmental situation in which it finds itself. Its behavior is definitely determined from without.

On the other hand, consider the *thermostat*. Here is an instrument with all the characteristics of the thermometer *plus* one enormously significant factor—namely, the element of control. It responds to its environment, and then, if the temperature does not correspond with the particular degree designated by the standard set by the thermostat itself, the said thermostat immediately puts into operation certain unapparent, but potent, forces which change the outside temperature and make it conform to the "ideal" maintained by the pointer on the calibration of the thermostat. If the house, church or school, for example, is too cold—that is, if the temperature falls below the standard suggested by the thermostat —the furnace fires are started, the radiators heated, and the rooms are warmed to the desired temperature. And when that degree is attained, the furnace is shut off. Then, too, in a properly air-conditioned area, whenever the weather is too hot, the cooling system is put in operation and the temperature is brought down to the prescribed degree. The environment is determined by the thermostat, not vice versa.

Is there not sufficient suggestiveness in these two symbols to warrant some valid generalizations concerning the nature of the world's struggle? Basically, it would seem that there are but two principles of earthly existence: one, we might say, of survival; another, of progress. Naturally, they have much in common; in innumerable ways they are subtly interfused and almost indistinguishable. But there is a fundamental difference between them.

The thermometric principle, let us say, is that of *adjustment* or *adaptation* to external exigencies and environment. This is the dominant characteristic of all subhuman life. All organisms of the lower order, all plants and animals, survive largely by their capacity to adapt themselves to their surroundings. The Darwinian theory of the survival of the fittest (not the "fightingest") is the scientific elaboration of this contention. The organisms which can most readily and thoroughly adjust themselves to changing conditions last the longest. Conversely, those species die out that cannot conform to the inherent demands of an altered environment. Obviously, therefore, a high premium is placed upon flexibility, easy adjustment, ready willingness to change one's very nature, if necessary. In all subhuman exsitence, survival value largely depends upon the ability to be conformed to this world.

But eventually, in the long evolutionary process, a creature comes into existence into whom God Almighty breathed His own eternal spirit, and he becomes a living soul—a man. This distinguishing characteristic that marks him off from the animal may well be called his thermostatic capacity. For although this creature has all sorts of animal qualities, he has something uniquely additional—he is made in the image of his Creator. That is, he is endowed with creative capacity; he is more than a creature, he is a co-creator potentially. In man is a new factor—*control*. He has imagination. He can dream dreams and see visions of what ought to be. He has the power to reason, to believe, to act on vast assumptions. He can contact illimitable resources of power, and put them into effective operation. Instead of being *conformed* to this world, he can *transform* it. Refusing to be determined by his environment, he can determine what it shall be. In terms of a heavenly vision he can build a new earth—if he will. For when he is what his Maker obviously intended him to be, he is not a thermometer; he is a thermostat.

To be sure, there are limitations to man's power. He cannot make the moon stand still, nor push the stars around—yet. But give him time. It is astounding to see how he is constantly extending the area of his control, particularly in the physical realm. The New York World's Fair was a rather impressive display of his achievements in this sphere—even though the present world debacle bears tragic testimony to his power to prostitute his accomplishments to destructive ends. But after all the necessary qualifications have been made, one generalization seems amply justified: if we would make progress, and not merely attempt to survive, we must live far more wholeheartedly in terms of our thermostatic capacities, rather than our thermometric ones.

The outworking of these contrasting principles is readily discernible in virtually all the major areas of interest. Consider some of the ramifications in at least four significant realms.

First of all, is it not fair to say that from the standpoint of social behavior there are two easily recognized types of persons *People* who might well be designated as thermometers and thermostats? The former are those who act as though their chief object in life is to do whatever is "being done." Their major passion is to be popular with the crowd or at least with their own "set." Chameleonlike, they change their color according to their surroundings. Any uniqueness is abhorrent to them. They think, act, live according to the dictates of custom. Their manner of dress is dictated by the fashion or the fad of the day. Their conversation is composed of conventional clichés. They mouth the hackneyed catch phrases popular for the season. Their pleasures are arbitrarily determined by the unimaginative amusement makers who invent some stupid new vogue in entertainment, or revive some antique diversion and adorn it in modern disguise. Those most devoid of individuality and the deadest in manner they consider most fashionable. Their first and final justification for doing anything is the silly statement "everybody is doing it." They ridicule genuine enthusiasm, hate originality, are horrified at independent action. If cocktails and bridge are the rage, no matter how much they hate either or both, they drink and play by night and by day. They have no convictions save the insane belief that to succeed one must conform.

To be sure, in any ordered society there are certain tacit agreements that all decent and respectable persons recognize which compel considerable conformity and even universal observance. Laws to enforce such common action are necessary and wise, particularly when the welfare of all may be jeopardized by the anti-social behavior of a few. But this is not the point at issue. It is not intelligent co-operation we deplore, but ignorant, uncritical, cowardly conformity.

Human thermometers are those who are unaware of a far more fundamental law which declares that whoever gauges and models himself after the crowd is on the road to deterioration and eventual ruin; that all real moral advancement and true success is solitary and along "the lone trail."

Charles Kingsley once wrote an open letter to the young men of his parish. The first paragraph ought to be memorized by young and old of both sexes. It began:

My dear Young Men:
The human race may for practical purposes be divided into three divisions. First, the honest men who mean to do right, and do it; second, the knaves who mean to do wrong, and do it; third, the fools who mean to do whichever of the two is pleasanter at the moment. And these last may be divided into black fools and white fools. The black fools are they who would rather do wrong than right, but dare not unless it is the fashion; while the white fools are they who would rather do right than wrong, but dare not unless it is the fashion.

Fools—human thermometers; virtually synonymous. And how many there are in the world! People who are so little above the animal level in character development. The herd instinct still dominates them. Each is subtly bulldozed by what's "being done." The fad flogs them into conformity. This lad gets to drinking because he does not like to refuse "the gang." Another degrades himself just trying to keep step.

When the devil was cast out of the Gadarene swine he confessed his name was "Legion." Demonic forces invariably get themselves wrapped up in the mob. And speaking generally, whenever a man surrenders his mind to the will of the crowd and marches along with the multitude, he is on his way to hell.

The saviors of the world are the thermostats. For the real gist of any kind of genuine salvation, Jew or Gentile, Catholic or Protestant, is that a man has formed a partnership of two—himself and God—against the world and all that dwell therein. Saving one's soul is, in its last essence, a sort of declaration of independence, a sworn allegiance to one's inner, individual convictions and ideals and renunciation of all outside authority. Invariably the strong characters, the leaders, the men who most effectively direct the destinies of the world, are men of conviction, creative independence and moral idealism, who point the finger of their purpose at those inner standards of what they think is right, and live in terms of them *quand meme*—in spite of everything. They are not molded by their environment. They mold it. Linked with invisible forces, they somehow release those powers with such efficacy as to change the moral atmosphere, generate new influences and transform an entire community.

In the Book of Books there is a very authentic description of the difference between the social behavior of those human thermometers and thermostats. The former are the many who crowd through the wide gate and down the broad way "that leadeth to destruction." The latter are the idealistic, independent, courageous few who with discrimination and determination go in at the strait gate and proceed down the narrow way "that leadeth to eternal life."

In the second place, the deep difference between these two principles of life is dramatically revealed in the *political* arena of our tense and tragic modern world. Underlying the contemporary carnival of carnage is the conflict of two gigantic, contradictory assumptions. On one assumption there has been builded, with sinister, spurious success, a political philosophy commonly called dictatorship. That form of government assumes that virtually all men are thermometers, that they will change with the conditions into which they are put, that they can be bulldozed, browbeaten and broken by simply "putting on the heat." When, for example, a whole people have been demoralized by defeat, starvation and a sense of utter inadequacy and despair, they are pretty much reduced to the level of the brute. Along comes an inflammatory demagogue who arouses their passions, stirs up their hatred, fires the desire for revenge, diverts their attention from their own impotency by pointing out a scapegoat on whom they can put the blame for all their failures, appeals to their sadistic natures one moment and to their national egotism another, insists that if they but give him unquestioning obedience, accept his orders without hesitancy or criticism, goose-step, drill and drudge as he directs, he will conquer the world.

And he seems to succeed for a time—but at what a cost! And how ephemeral are his victories! For when men revert to the animal they may be able to destroy, but they cannot build anything of enduring strength. Creativity dies out. Independent thought expires. The God in them is suffocated. Then the beast in them is unleashed, and they begin to lay waste a world. They are told that through totalitarianism, the surrender of everything to the state, they shall find a new freedom. But it is all a lie. The end is merciless tyranny, slavery and disintegration worse than death.

But there is an opposing assumption, as daring as it is divine, and on it is based the political philosophy of democracy. This form of government assumes that all men are potentially thermostats—not yet actually, by any means (which accounts for democracy's major difficulties), but latently, capable of becoming such. Thus the state exists for the individual, not the individual for the state, and the test of democracy's strength is to be found in its ability to develop and enrich human personality, not merely among the privileged few, but in every last boy and girl throughout the land. The state guaranteeing the rights of the individual,

and the individual recognizing his responsibility to the state, it is possible, we contend, to achieve greater liberty, more creative co-operation, higher culture, more lasting happiness and nobler living than in any other way. Therefore, in order that each individual may make the most of his best for the sake of the rest, he must become a thermostat—to do his own thinking, to express his own convictions, to adhere to his highest ideals and to obey God rather than man. And to the degree that we do this, to that degree does democracy thrive and fulfill the hopes and dreams of those who established our nation and set up a Constitution limiting the powers of the state and guaranteeing to all the indispensable rights of free speech, press, assembly and religious worship. But when, for any reason, we become mob-minded, fearful of personal responsibility, or so secularized that we lose contact with God and put all our faith in mammon or Mars—in short, when we become thermometers, then is democracy most surely threatened with doom.

A third area of interest in which these conflicting principles are vigorously operative is that of _education_. Here, as everywhere, there are points of coalescence, but for the most part the difference is fairly clear and determinative. Thermometric education, so to speak, is counterfeit, spurious, false. It invariably stresses indoctrination, regimentation, uncritical acceptance of any ideas those in authority present. Its basic techniques are those of the propagandist, every one of which is anathema to a true education.

The only valid education is that which we may call thermostatic. It seeks to develop insight, discrimination, critical judgment, the capacity to weigh values, recognize truth, distinguish between right and wrong, beauty and ugliness, liberty and license. Its main objective is the development of full-orbed, balanced, dynamic personalities that dare to be their unique selves in order that they might contribute to the welfare of all the one ingredient each alone can give—individuality. Not mere cleverness, but character; not only great skill, but likewise goodwill; not simply discipline, but deliverance from frustration, folly and futility—in short, great living is what thermostatic education seeks to develop.

⁴ "Religion"

Finally, consider the two basic types of _religion_—again, thermometric versus thermostatic. Says the former, "What cannot be cured, must be endured. Whatever is, must be. Learn to adjust yourself. Be resigned to the inevitable. All evil comes from individual desire. Therefore learn to extirpate it. For when desire is destroyed you will become a part of the vast nothingness, the flame of life will die out, the ultimate emancipation will be achieved—you will attain Nirvana." The emphasis of such religion, you see, is an escape, avoidance of struggle and the denial of individuality. Its major symbol is a wheel—the wheel of rebirth—rolling down the line of least resistance. And it develops both an indifference and a degree of immunity to social wrongs, economic injustice, political tyranny and the other major evils of this world. A passive, silent, hands-in-lap, unseeing Buddha is its incarnation, and an unprogressive civilization is its outworking.

But there is a thermostatic type of religion, thank God, and its highest expression is called vital Christianity. It makes quite contrary declarations and demands. "What cannot be endured, must be cured," it insists. "What is, must be judged in the light of the Christ ideal, and made over into what ought to be. Don't conform to this world, transform it! Your desires are God-given. Discipline them, direct them toward the highest you know, that they may drive you to your goal. Deny your petty, egocentric self, that you find your greatest, most Godlike self. Lose your life for His sake, that you might really save it. Yours is the world, make it over into the Kingdom of Heaven. You can do all things through Christ who strengtheneth you! When you see the trend of affairs going in the wrong direction, fling your life across it and redirect it. The symbol of Christianity is a Cross!" This is the religion that redeems the world.

One final suggestion. Confronted with the towering problems of our modern day, every sincere person sooner or later asks himself some such question as this: "But what can I do? I, a tiny, human unit in a world so vast and wicked?" Well, each can at least do this much. Remember that this world of ours is not a mechanism, as the materialists assert. It is an organism, a growing thing. To cure its evils is not a matter of tinkering with an intricate machine, requiring a new engine, relined brakes, a gadget here and an adjustment there. It is a matter of seed-sowing, of sunshine and rain, of proper cultivation, and pre-eminently of the right atmosphere. Therefore, sow the right seed, function as a thermostat. Linked with the infinite resources of God, you can release them to unbelievable advantage. Setting the pointer of your purpose at the standard designated by your Christ, you can do as he commands you regardless of the lure of the crowd or the temptation of the devil. Then you need not worry or fret. God, through you, will warm the bitter, frigid earth until the decencies and virtues can grow again, and the desert blossom as the rose.

One little Jew, more effectively than any other, did just that. He changed the world. And he left the secret of his success in a simple all-wise suggestion: "Be not conformed to this world: but be ye transformed by the renewing of your mind, that ye may prove what is that good, and acceptable, and perfect, will of God!" Be not thermometers—be thermostats!

# 4

# The Priesthood of the Laity

## By LOUIS H. EVANS

I DOUBT IF THERE IS A MORE PATHETIC PICTURE IN HISTORY than that which is in the 5th chapter of John's Gospel. A paralytic on one hand and healing power and restoration on the other. There is only one thing lacking—no laymen to help him in! A world-paralytic frustrated, tired, war-torn and afraid! Here the healing waters. Here the helpless one. "But I have no man when the water is troubled to help me in." One layman lacking!

There was a cry outside a city wall two thousand years ago, "Finished," and something happened. "The veil of the Temple was rent from the top to the bottom." Now what was that veil of the Temple? It was something that kept the laymen out of the presence of God. Behind it there stood the Ark of the Covenant with its light symbolizing the presence of God. The priests could go in and out ministering, but not the laymen. Two tried it and they were stricken dead. But something happened at Calvary. You and I suddenly had access to God by faith in Christ and his Cross. Before that it meant death to any layman to come into the

*Louis H. Evans is the Minister-at-large of the Board of National Missions of the Presbyterian Church, U.S.A. He served previously as the pastor of the First Presbyterian Church, Hollywood, California.*

presence of God. Now no layman even begins to live until he does. As Paul said, from that hour on you are all of the royal priesthood of God, laymen and clergy. John says ye are the *cleros*— the clergy of God. In all truth, every layman wears his robe. Every Christian woman is a priestess of the Royal Order of God.

Now the great revivals of the world have struck us for the most part when laymen have conceived of their great place. In the Old Testament Amos said, "I am not a prophet nor the son of a prophet. I am a tender of sycamore vines." He was a rancher. But God said, "Speak to the people," and he spoke. Then it happened. Robert Speer, one of the greatest laymen the Church has ever known, shook the world. Billy Sunday, the evangelist, was a professional ball player. D. L. Moody was a shoe clerk. Dr. Finney, the great evangelist, was a college president. Not all this dynamic consecration belonged to the cloth and fortunate has been that generation when there has been a revival of obligation and spirit on the part of the laity.

It was a great day for missions one day when Carey put over his shoe cobbling shop, "Carey, cobbler for the grace of God." Someone remonstrated with him saying, "Carey, you are spending too much time in religious work; you are neglecting your business." Carey said, "Gentlemen, I cobble shoes to earn my bread and butter. My business is to serve God."

Every one of us has a single vocation. Should this cryptic question be addressed to you, "Sir, what is your vocation?" What would you say? Not, "We are butchers, bakers, candlestick makers, doctors, lawyers," but rather, "We seek first the kingdom of God and its righteousness. That is our vocation, Sir."

"Thy kingdom come" was explained in the next phrase as we spoke it tonight: "Thy will be done on earth, as it is in heaven." To this cause every one of us was born. To see that Christ is so sovereign in the hearts of men that we have a kingdom on earth. A fraternity or a sorority of goodness, fairness, honesty, justice and love. However a man may make his living, this is what he is living for. This is it. No man begins to live till he catches that. A blacksmith's bellows breathes, but it does not live, and a lot of folk breathe, but they do not live.

Now, a man's profession happens to be the particular tool he has chosen to bring the Kingdom to come to pass in his own particular way. The Kingdom is simple a group of men and women all of one "vocation" wearing the varied colored garbs of different "professions" but with one driving pulsing passion, the Kingdom of God.

Now, that has to do, of course, with the human equation. It was Roger Babson who said, "The best people agree that the preeminent object for which all banks, governments, factories, schools, stores exist, is to make people healthier and happier."

If you and I have had a religious experience, it must evidence itself in everything we do. Above all we must never divorce our profession from our vocation. I was giving some addresses in Idaho State College a few years ago when a Navy official asked me if I wouldn't like to come and visit the ordnance factory. I said I would. He showed me those twelve- and fourteen-inch guns and enough electrical aiming and firing gadgets to rearm every ship in the navy. As I gazed at these death-dealing instruments, I asked him, "Captain, are you going to use these things someday?" He said, "Evans, that's not my business, that's up to you religionists." I said, "Wait a minute, sir. You can't 'pass the buck' to me that way." You see what he was doing? By profession he was a navy man, by vocation he forgot he was a Kingdom-of-God-man. He thought he could work all week on navy guns and sleep in on Sunday morning while I got up and tried to implement the hearts of men with this Kingdom idea.

You know, it is a pathetic thing when a man is so busy making a living, he forgets what he is living for; when he is so utterly engrossed in his profession, he has forgotten his vocation. That is dangerous in the realm of science. A man must use his profession then as a means of this inner higher spiritual expression. As someone said, "Any religious experience which surely saves a man, must get into his social relationships. If what has happened to him doesn't make him a better husband, a more conscientious citizen, a more generous employer, a more dependable and honest employee, then he has not been saved, he has only been emotionalized." No man is truly saved till this Kingdom passion has possessed him, for to this end was he born.

A good many laymen are coming to a new appraisal of their task endeavoring to spiritualize it. One thing I know, in this particular job that happens to be mine now, is the number of Chambers of Commerce that in their annual banquets want a talk on "God." You men have noticed it at luncheon clubs. A few years ago you could get by with "three wisecracks and a filler" and sit down; but not any more. Men want to come to grips with deeper things, and organizations of employers or employees are trying honestly to spiritualize the tasks which they do.

This is certainly true of science. I suppose we have no more enthusiastic evangelists for the spiritualities today than some scientists. What that college president said was true: "I look about me and I am frightened. Our minds run our hearts and I am sick to death of engineering." Somehow if our technology is not mastered by spiritual motivation, it will be hard for us. Charles Lindbergh said some time ago that he used to be a disciple of man and science. He said science is our shepherd, but now he realized science was not a shepherd. Science was just a tool and it needs the guidance of the spirit in a day like this or we shall destroy ourselves.

Education too is becoming spiritual. No longer are we interested merely in the technologies. What young people *know* today is not quite as important now on the campus as how they *feel,* for it is doubtful if we dare know any more without feeling rightly. There the teacher has an unusual opportunity for spiritual maturation in a day of a new nostalgia for God in education.

Subjects now, on the campus, are less an end than they are just a means to that end. There was a certain father who was accosted by a professor who said, "Your son flunked in grammar." The father replied, "I'm sorry, but I want to thank you for something else you have done for my boy; you've given him a great spiritual, altruistic aim and purpose in life. You see, sir, as a father, this is my idea of education: I would rather my boy would come out of your class saying 'I seed' when he had seen, than to say 'I saw' when he had never seen at all." What good is grammar unless our young people have something to say? What good is art unless there is something spiritual to splash on canvas? What's the use of singing if you have no message to sing? Why learn to speak if you have nothing to say?

One day a boy scribbled something on a paper and handed it to the girl with braids in front of him and it read "I love you." He spelled it "luv." He felt rightly, but he spelled wrongly. The next day he wrote another note, "I hate you," and he handed it to a boy across the aisle. He spelled it "hate." He spelled rightly, but he felt wrongly. Now, if you had to choose between two types of education, one that made you spell rightly, but permitted you to feel wrongly, or an educational system that permitted you to spell wrongly, but insisted that you feel rightly, which would you choose? Let's have both. The National Education Association said some time ago, "Man hungers and thirsts after righteousness . . . and the great universe calls to his spirit and unless he willfully closes his ears, he hears the voice of God. . . No greater task rests upon the secondary school than to help its pupils find their God. How this is to be done is the greatest of problems. Of one thing only we are sure, we cannot solve this problem by ignoring it." We see great movements now in education where the spirit insists on catching up with the brain.

This is also true in medicine. You ladies and gentlemen who have that as your professon find it closely knitted now to your vocational purpose, which is the Kingdom of God and spiritualities, do you not? One doctor said to me some time ago, "You know, Evans, if I am going to be a good surgeon, a good doctor, I must know three subjects—physiology, mental therapeutics and religion." I asked, "Why religion?" He answered, "Because the body and soul live so closely together, they catch each other's diseases." That is true. He said, "When I go into a sickroom, I have to realize that sometimes that man needs a promise more than he needs a pill. And before I can cure that fever, I must quench the fear that is causing the fever."

When the great Dr. Sladen, with 140 doctors under him at Ford Hospital in Detroit, came to Pittsburgh to address the surgeons, they allowed me to remain in the room while he was giving his address and I shall never forget what he said: "Gentlemen, in medicine you and I must need, in a day like this when men are cracking up all about us, something more than you can buy in the corner pharmacies. We need a great grip on God." Then he went on to explain. He said nine other surgeons and he, who had been appointed by the United States government, were asked to draw up ten laws of public health and give them to the American people. He said, "We debated and argued from ten to twelve days and finally one of us decided, 'Let's take the beatitudes of Jesus Christ.' " He said then, "We cut the laws down to nine and we simply changed the word 'blessed' to 'healthy' and we had it." "Healthy are the pure in heart," because sin is sand in the human machinery and it shakes a man to pieces. "Healthy are the peacemakers" because hatred brings about a schizophrenia and a divided personality inside that tears us to pieces—in disposition, in health and in power. They had it—the laws of the Nazarene!

The same thing is true in industry. You men know enough now

about capital and labor to realize that "out of the heart are the issues of life" and both capital and labor need regeneration. One day a financial expert was asked to visit and look over a factory that was going to pieces in both profits and personnel. He studied it carefully. Now, this financial expert could not be properly defined, as someone defined a financial expert, as being a man who had a Tau Kappa Alpha key at one end of his chain, but no watch at the other! He knew his business. After he had studied this factory for some months, he called them all together from the chairman of the board of directors, management, sales manager, managers of labor, to the last man that worked at the lathe. He said, "Gentlemen, what this factory needs is conversion." Immediately the president of the board spoke up and said, "We are converting our machinery, sir, from wartime to peacetime machines." He said, "I did not say the conversion of *machinery*. This factory needs a conversion of its *men*. From the president of the board of trustees to the last man who works at the lathe, you are all rotten with selfishness and unless you can find God, you can expect ruin in both personnel and profits." How true that is. You and I know that the maintaining or the rescinding of the Taft-Hartley Law will be scarcely more than treating the pimples on the skin when the blood is bad. Deep within lie the causes of unrest and out of the heart are the issues of life. To be sure, some of our greatest prophets now are men in the sphere of industry.

The same thing is true in the realm of business. I do not mean that monetary considerations are not important. They are. Someone said in one of the presidential elections, "I don't know for the life of me whether to vote for a Republican and go to the poorhouse or vote for a Democrat and continue to build them." It seems to be a "toss up." There are monetary and budgetary considerations. But do you call this success in business, gentlemen, when Mr. Babson said, "Ninetenths of the investors are in search, not of a way to curb periods of over expansion and wasteful depressions that hurt people, but rather of a way to hold their securities up to the very day that the market breaks in order to unload them in the nick of time on someone less fortunate than themselves." That couldn't possibly be it, could it? The Christian businessman has something more to offer us than this, for "the abundance of life consists not merely in the abundance of things that a man possesses."

In the year 1923 in Chicago's Edgewater Beach Hotel there sat six businessmen: the president of the largest steel corporation in the world, a member of the President's cabinet, the greatest bear on Wall Street, the president of the New York Stock Exchange, the president of the Bank of the International Settlement, and the greatest wheat speculator in the world. These six tycoons possessed more money than was in the whole United States Treasury combined. They were the men that the magazines played up as men of Success, with a capital "S." Departments of economics in colleges and universities held them up as the acme of success.

Twenty-five years passed. What happened to these six men? The president of the largest steel company in the world died dead broke. Another one of the men was released recently from Sing Sing Penitentiary. Another man was pardoned from prison, so he could die at home. The fourth man committed suicide. The fifth man committed suicide. The sixth man committed suicide. These men knew how to make *money*, but did they know how to make a *life*? That is not success! Today in the realm of business there is a hunger and a thirst for something more than this Tyrian stuff that slips through our fingers too easily.

The same thing is true now in the military. I shall never forget several hours I spent in the Pentagon some time ago. They discussed the hydrogen bomb and walking down the Pentagon corridor with one of the admirals, he said to me, pointing to his heart, "The trouble is all here." MacArthur started it by saying,

"This is a theological war," and "There's nothing more the military can do. It has had its last chance." And it has. You don't change men by "punching their nose in." Mr. Eisenhower said, "Every dollar we spend on guns and battleships is robbing some-one of God and bread. When can we stop making these iron crosses?" The top brass of the military is saying the same thing, "When can we stop making these crosses? There's nothing more that we can do." All war ever did was to act as an anesthetic to "knock out" Germany and Japan, strap them to the table and then call for Christian people with the therapeutics of God and the regenerative power of the spirit to operate, cutting out these cancerous ideologies. Unless we do that, when the patient convalesces, he will be just as bad as before we "knocked him out" with a trillion dollar war "anesthetic," forgetting to operate with the tools of the Spirit.

It was my privilege not long ago to be at Ridgecrest, North Carolina, where the Air Force tried its first spiritual experiment of this type. They invited military leaders and personnel from all over America; thought if they had five hundred it would be wonderful. A thousand gathered for five days to pray and talk about God. You and I are living in the day when the militarist is becoming an evangelist. Listen to Omar Bradley saying, "We have too many men of science, too few men of God. We are a nation of nuclear giants and spiritual infants. We've taught our young men more about how to kill than what they are living for." It is God we need now. Listen to the centurion in armor speak—he is becoming a priest too in his own right.

What an awakening in the home too. The home is "a solar system"; we realize that now. The sun is at the center of the solar system; put anything less at the center and it flies to pieces. The reason the American home goes to pieces lies in the fact that the average home has no great central spiritual solar sun . . . the Son of God. And when you know that one out of three

American homes is broken by divorce, you come to realize statistically, factually and functionally that Jesus Christ is a great "adhesive"—he holds the home together. Now universities are installing for the first time courses on the home with a very definite religious intonation.

After all, the greatest contribution a woman makes in the home is in the task of "priestess." Not merely in the culinary art, as a seamstress, a nurse, or as a companion, but in the spiritual contribution she makes to those who bear her name and him whom she loves. I think one of the greatest tributes to a wife ever made was written in these lines:

I love you not only for what you are, but for what I am when I am with you. I love you not only for what you have made of yourself, but for what you are making of me. I love you for that part of me that you bring out. I love you for putting your hand into my heaped up heart and passing over all the foolish, weak things you can't help seeing there and for drawing out into the light all the beautiful longings no one else had looked quite long enough to find. I love you because you are helping me to make of the lumber of my life not a tavern, but a temple.

In every phase of life someone wants to feel he or she is having a part in this royal, spiritual priesthood and that it lies within the functions and the confines of our possibilities. You and I as Christians with the regenerative power of Christ and the Holy Spirit as our token possession, realize that we can lead a paralyzed world to its healing fountains. We thank God for this confidence and we look at the world from a curative standpoint. Something can be done about it! While other humans are so despairingly saying, "See what this world is coming to," you and I with confidence look up and remember our spiritual tools and are saying, "See who had come to this world!" Christ is sufficient.

Whenever you and I are impatient with humanity, let us remember the patient God of impatient men and realize that in building and reshaping the human heart, the human society, we are not dealing with mushrooms; we are dealing with century plants. If you become impatient with those you know in the particular area of life that you are trying to spiritualize, then how would you like to be God? Many times when I have become somewhat discouraged with my humble task, I like to read these words of Badger Clark in his poem, "The Job," and I would like to suggest in closing that we make them ours in prayer:

> But, God, it won't come right! it won't come right!
> I've worked it over till my brain is numb.
> The first flash came so bright,
> Then more ideas after it—flash! flash!—I thought it some
> New constellation men would wonder at.
> Perhaps it's just a firework—flash! fizz! spat!
> Then darker darkness and scorched pasteboard and sour smoke.
>
> But, God, the thought was great,
> The scheme, the dream—why, till the first charm broke
> The thing just built itself while I, elate,
> Laughed and admired it. Then it stuck,
> Half done, the lesser half, worse luck!
> You see, it's dead as yet, a frame, a body—and the heart,
> The soul, the fiery vital part
> To give it life is what I cannot get. I've tried—
> You know it—tried to catch live fire
> And pawed cold ashes. Every spark has died.
> It won't come right! I'd drop the thing entire,
> Only—I can't! I love my job.
>
> You, who ride the thunder,
> Do you know what it is to dream and drudge and throb?
> I wonder.
> Did it come at you with a rush, your dream, your plan?
> If so, I know how you began.
> Yes, with rapt face and sparkling eyes,
> Swinging the hot globe out between the skies,

Marking the new seas with their white beach lines,
Sketching in sun and moon, the lightning and the rains,
Sowing the hills with pines,
Wreathing a rim of purple round the plains.
I know you laughed then, while you caught and wrought
The big, swift, rapturous outline of your thought.
And then—
Men!
I see it now.
O God, forgive my pettish row.
I see your job. While ages crawl
Your lips take laboring lines, your eyes a sadder light,
For man, the fire and flower and center of it all—
Man won't come right!
After your patient centuries,
Fresh starts, recastings, tired Gethsemanes
And tense Golgothas, he, your central theme
Is just a jangling echo of your dream.
Grand as the rest may be, he ruins it.

Why don't you quit?
Crumple it all and dream again! But no;
Flaw after flaw, you work it out, revise, refine—
Bondage, brutality, and war, and woe,
The sot, the fool, the tyrant and the mob—
Dear God, how you must love your job!
Help me, as I love mine.[1]

[1] From *Sky Lines and Wood Smoke* by Badgar Clark. Used by permission of the author.

# 5

# The Importance of Doubting Our Doubts

## By HARRY EMERSON FOSDICK

IN THE VOCABULARY OF RELIGION THE WORD "DOUBT" HAS A bad significance. Have you ever heard a preacher use it in a favorable sense? Faith is the great word. Faith is the victory that overcomes the world, and is not doubt its chief enemy? So the word "doubt" has been exiled to religion's semantic doghouse.

But that does not solve the problem. Once more, facing this audience, I feel what I commonly feel when I face worshiping congregations. You look so pious. You are so reverent. You listen so respectfully to scripture and anthem. You sing so earnestly the resounding hymns. Yet I know and you know that in every life here is something else which our worship does not express—doubts, questions, uncertainties, skepticism. Every one of us, facing the Christian faith, must honestly say what the man in the Gospel story said to Jesus: "Lord, I believe; help thou mine unbelief." Especially, in these days, so disturbing to placid, docile faith about God and man, how applicable are the Bishop's words in Browning's poem:

*Harry Emerson Fosdick is pastor emeritus of Riverside Church, New York City.*

With me, faith means perpetual unbelief
Kept quiet like the snake 'neath Michael's foot,
Who stands calm just because he feels it writhe.

Concerning this problem, which in one way or another we all face, I offer two preliminary observations. First, doubt is not a "snake"; the capacity to doubt is one of man's noblest powers. Look at our world today and see the innumerable beliefs and practices, from communism up and down, which ought to be doubted! The great servants of our race have been distinguished by the fact that in the face of universally accepted falsehoods they dared stand up and cry: I doubt that! Without the capacity to doubt there could be no progress—only docile, unquestioning acceptance of the status quo and its established dogmatisms.

Think of the scientific realm! The earth is flat, the sun circles round it—when such ideas were everywhere accepted, a few bravely dared to disbelieve them. Every scientific advance has started with skepticism. When we think of the scientific pioneers we emphasize their faith, their affirmative belief in new ideas and possibilities. Right! But in the experience of the pioneers themselves their first poignant struggle, their initial critical venture, centered in perilous and daring disbelief. Galileo was right when he called doubt the father of discovery.

But—someone says—when we turn from science to religion, we want faith—faith in God, in Christ, in the human soul. Of course we want faith! But anyone who thinks he can achieve great faith without exercising his God-given capacity to doubt, is oversimplifying the problem. Jesus himself was a magnificent doubter. Wild ideas of a war-making Messiah who would overthrow Rome were prevalent in his time. He doubted them. "An eye for an eye and tooth for a tooth" was the true law, they said. He doubted it. He saw men trusting in long prayers, broad phylacteries, rigid Sabbath rules, dietary laws as essential to true religion, and he doubted them all. He saw men believing in ancient traditions just because they were ancient, and he poured his skepticism on such reactionaries: "It was said unto them of old time, but I say unto you." Samaritans are an inferior race was the popular idea, but he scorned it; a good Samaritan, he said, is better than a bad priest. We are saved by Jesus' faith, we say. Yes, but just as truly as any scientific pioneer did, he reached his faith through his daring doubts. My friends, we sing the praises of the great believers. So do I! But who can worthily express our unpayable indebtedness to the brave doubters, who in perilous times, when false ideas dominated men's minds and spoiled their lives, saved the day with their courageous disbelief? Let us sing their praises too!

To someone here, struggling with this problem, I am saying first: Don't despise your capacity to doubt! Honor it! It is one of your noblest attributes.

My second preliminary observation is that the sturdiest faith has always come out of the struggle with doubt. There are only two ways in which we can possess Christian faith. One is to inherit it, borrow it, swallow it without question, take it over as we do the cut of our clothes without thinking about it. Some here may be able to do that, but your faith then is not really *yours*. You never fought for it. As one student said: "Being a Methodist, just because your parents were, is like wearing a secondhand hat that does not fit." No! Great faith, if it is really to be one's very own, always has to be fought for.

One who does not understand this, does not understand the Bible. It is a book of faith, we say. To be sure it is! But it is also a book filled with the struggles of men wrestling with their doubts and unbelief. Listen to Gideon crying, "If the Lord is with us, why then has all this befallen us?" Listen to the Psalmist:

> My tears have been my food day
> and night,

> While they continually say unto me,
>     Where is thy God?

Listen to Job complaining to God:

> I cry unto thee, and thou dost not answer me,

or to Jeremiah calling God "a deceitful brook" and "waters that fail," and crying,

> Cursed be the day on which I was born!

The Bible only a book of faith? But listen to Ecclesiastes: "Vanity of vanities, all is vanity. . . . That which befalleth the sons of men befalleth beasts . . . as the one dieth, so dieth the other; yea, they have all one breath; and man hath no pre-eminence above the beasts." Indeed, listen to our Lord himself on Calvary! He is quoting the twenty-second Psalm. He knows it by heart:

> My God, my God, why hast thou
>     forsaken me?
> Why art thou so far from
>     helping me?

I am talking to someone here who is struggling with his doubts. The Bible is your book, my friend. All its faith was hammered out on the hard anvil of doubt.

The trouble is that most Christians know about the faith of the great believers but not about their inner struggles. All Yale men here, and many more of us too, remember William Lyon Phelps. What a radiant Christian faith he had! But listen to him in his autobiography: "My religious faith remains in possession of the field only after prolonged civil war with my naturally sceptical mind." That experience belongs in the best tradition of the great believers. John Knox, the Scottish Reformer—what a man of conviction! Yes, but remember that time when his soul knew "anger, wrath and indignation, which it conceived against God, calling all his promises in doubt." Increase Mather—that doughty Puritan—what a man of faith! Yes, but read his diary and run on entries like this: "Greatly molested with temptations to atheism." Sing Luther's hymn, "A mighty fortress is our God," and one would suppose he never questioned his faith, but see him in other hours. "For more than a week," he wrote, "Christ was wholly lost. I was shaken by desperation and blasphemy against God."

I speak for the encouragement of some one here struggling with his unbelief. The noblest faith of the Church has come out of that struggle. No man really possesses the Christian faith until he has fought for it. So Browning put it:

> The more of doubt, the stronger faith, I say,
> If faith o'ercomes doubt.

That brings us to the vital issue. How does faith overcome doubt?

Today I emphasize one central matter in the experience of the great believers: they went honestly through with their disbeliefs until at last they began to doubt their doubts. How important that process is! When it was first suggested that steamships could be built which would cross the ocean, multitudes were skeptical. One man proved it could not be done. He wrote a book proving that no steamship could carry enough fuel to keep its engines going across the ocean. Well, the first steamship that crossed the Atlantic and landed in New York Harbor carried a copy of that book. Ah, my skeptical disbeliever, you would have been a wiser man had you carried your doubts a little further until you doubted your doubts! I am preaching this sermon because I want someone here not to stop doubting, but to go through with his skepticism until he disbelieves his disbelief.

Let us apply this first to our faith in God! Someone here is struggling with doubts about God. Well, there are many ideas of God which ought to be doubted. The Bible itself progresses from one discarded idea of God to a nobler concept of Him because men dared to doubt. But when it comes to surrendering belief in God and becoming an atheist, have you ever carried your doubts through to *that* conclusion? See where that lands you! No God! Nothing ultimately creative here except protons and electrons going it blind! All creation, as one atheist says, only "an accident in a backwater!" Everything explained by the chance collocation of physical elements! All the law-abiding order and beauty of the world, all the nobility of human character at its best, explained as though the physical letters of the alphabet had been blown together by a chance wind into the Thirteenth Chapter of First Corinthians! Christ himself and all he stands for—nothing, as it were, nothing but the physical notes of the musical scale tossed by purposeless winds until accidentally they fell together into the Ninth Symphony! Can you really believe that? Is not that utterly incredible?

In the United States today we face a strong trend back toward religious faith, and one reason, I think, lies in what we are saying now. Many in this last generation surrendered to skepticism, went through with it to its conclusion, until they began finding their disbelief unbelievable.

So Robert Louis Stevenson became a man of radiant faith, but he did not start that way. He started by calling the religion he was brought up in "the deadliest gag and wet-blanket that can be laid on man." He started by calling himself "a youthful atheist." Then, as he grew up, began what Gilbert Chesterton called his "first wild doubts of doubt." "The Church was not right," wrote Stevenson, "but certainly not the antichurch either." " 'Tis a strange world," he said, "but there is a manifest God for those who care to look for Him." Then at last he begins talking about his "cast-iron faith." "Whether on the first of January or the thirty-first of December," he writes, "faith is a good word to end on." So he went through with his skepticism until he found his disbelief unbelievable.

I thank God now that that experience of Stevenson's was mine too. When I started for college my junior year, I told my mother that I was going to clear God out of the universe and begin all over to see what I could find. I could not swallow the Christian faith unquestioningly. I had to fight for it. And so it's mine! Every doubt raised against it, every question asked about it, I have faced often with agony of mind. I am not afraid of atheism; of all my disbeliefs I most certainly disbelieve that! And now in my elder years what a Christian of the last generation said I understand: "Who never doubted never half believed."

Let us apply this truth now not only to faith in God but to faith in Christ. For many people he is hard to believe in now. Too good to be true! Too idealistic to fit this naughty world! So the idea creeps in that believers are credulous, gullible, soft-headed, trusting this lovely Christ with his lovely ideas as "the way, the truth and the life." Often on university campuses one runs upon this idea that to believe in Christ is comforting—yes!— but it takes a credulous mind to do it in a world like this. To which I say: Watch your step there! Again and again in history the shoe has been on the other foot. Not the believers in spiritual greatness, but the unbelievers have proved to be mistaken.

I thought of that when recently in Washington I stood before the Lincoln Memorial, saw again that noble figure seated there, and read on the carved stone the immortal words of the Gettysburg Address. A newspaper editor in Harrisburg, thirty-five miles away from Gettysburg, heard Lincoln's Gettyburg Address. Fall for that kind of stuff? Not he! He was no sucker! He was a hard-headed realist. So he wrote this in his paper: "We pass over the silly remarks of the President; for the credit of the nation, we are willing that the veil of oblivion shall be dropped over them and that they shall no more be repeated or thought of." Ah, you fool, you stood in the presence of greatness, and you disbelieved! It is you who were blind. It is you, the skeptic, at whom the centuries will laugh till the end of time. You doubted Lincoln. Why didn't you think twice, until you doubted your doubts?

The older I grow the more I ponder Judas Iscariot. He came so near to *not* betraying Jesus. He was a loyal disciple. It took courage to join that little band, and Judas had it. Then doubts began. What kind of Messiah was this who refused violent revolution and talked about loving one's enemies? Was not this idealistic Jesus letting them down? So the doubts grew, until in an explosive hour—oh, fifty-one votes against forty-nine—Judas sold his Lord. He came so near *not* doing it, that when he saw what he had done he hanged himself in shame. Ah, Judas, if you had only doubted your doubts enough to wait until Easter, until Pentecost, until Paul came, you would not be the supreme traitor of the centuries. You stood in the presence of divine greatness, and you disbelieved.

You see what I am trying to say. Believers can be credulous, but disbelievers too can be gullible fools. Don't join their company! Take a long look at Christ! The world desperately needs him. He is the way and the truth and the life.

Let us apply our theme now to faith in man and his possibilities. Here especially the pessimists are having a field day now. The Kingdom of God on earth—what a dream! What credulity it takes to believe that. On one of our campuses the college paper offered a prize for the best definition of life. Here are some that received honorable mention: "Life is a bad joke which isn't even funny." "Life is a disease for which the only cure is death." "Life is a jail sentence which we get for the crime of being born." My friends, when skepticism, not simply about religion but about human life, is thus carried to its logical conclusion, is it not about time to doubt our doubts?

You see, faith in God concerns something everlastingly so, whether we believe in it or not, but faith in man and his possibilities concerns something which may conceivably become so if we believe in it enough. Only if we have faith in human possibilities can they ever become real. If we all doubt them, they are dished. In this realm, faith is creative; doubt is destructive.

Well, are the skeptics about human hopes the wise egg-heads they think they are? Some time since I lectured at the University of Pittsburgh; and I recalled a man named Arthur Lee, who, in 1770, visited the present site of Pittsburgh and in his travel diary wrote this: "The place, I believe, will never be very considerable." There is the skeptic for you, multiplied millions of times in history, blind, blind as bats, to the possibilities which they lacked faith to see. Shakespeare was everlastingly right:

> Our doubts are traitors,
> And make us lose the good we oft might win,
> By fearing to attempt.

This truth which we are trying to make clear becomes most intimate when we apply it to our personal lives. God knows how many here today are burdened with the sense of failure—moral failure, it may be, so that they disbelieve in themselves and doubt that anything worth while can be made of their lives. Look at me, someone is saying, God would have to work a miracle to change me. Well, do you think that kind of miracle is incredible? Listen! I vividly recall the afternoon when I was well started on my radio sermon, when suddenly the man at the controls lifted his arms, and stopped me. "It's all off," he said, "the Japanese are attacking Pearl Harbor." What a day! Who can put into words the outraged thoughts we had about those Japanese bombers. My friends, the pilot who led the attack on Pearl Harbor is in this country now training to be a Christian missionary. He is Captain Mitsuo Fuchida, and he is going back to preach the gospel to his people. Incredible! one would have thought. No! That kind of miracle has made Christian history for nearly two thousand years. And *you* think that *you* cannot be transformed by the renewing of *your* mind. In God's name, doubt your doubts!

I call you to witness that today I have given doubt fair play. I have said in its favor, I think, the best that can be said. But in this tremendous generation we need men and women who have won through doubt to faith—faith in the possibilities of world organization, faith in interracial brotherhood and the abolition of war, faith in the Christian Church and its saving gospel, faith in what God can do in them and through them. I want someone here to come over now from skepticism to conviction. As John Masefield sang it:

> Oh yesterday our little troup
>     was ridden through and through,
> Our swaying, tattered pennons fled,
>     a broken, beaten few,
> And all the summer afternoon they
>     hunted us and slew;
> But tomorrow
> By the living God, we'll try the
>     game anew.[1]

That is faith! May we all doubt our doubts until we get it!

[1] "Tomorrow," from *Collected Poems* by John Masefield. Used by permission of The Macmillan Company.

# 6

## Waste, Want and Worthiness

### By J. WALLACE HAMILTON

I WANT TO LIFT UP THREE VERSES FROM THE PARABLE OF THE prodigal son: "He wasted his substance," "He began to be in want," "He said to his father, I am not worthy." Waste, want and worthiness.

This morning in Mound Park Hospital an eight-pound baby was born. He is one of the ten new arrivals expected in our city today, one of about three thousand anticipated—or as Winchell would say, "infanticipated"—in our city this year, one of three and a quarter million expected in America, one of twenty million in the world family. The stork is a busy bird. The world's population is increasing.

About three hundred years ago, for the first time as far as anyone knows, a world census was attempted and it was estimated then that, roughly, four hundred million people were living upon the earth. Then that number doubled and doubled again until today the estimate is over two and a half billion. Between now and tomorrow night the net gain of the stork over the grim reaper will be approximately fifty-five thousand.

We are assuming that this newly arrived citizen was born fully

*J. Wallace Hamilton is the pastor of the Pasadena Community Church, St. Petersburg, Florida.*

equipped with an appetite, a stomach and a healthy digestive
system, and that his first inaugural speech was a loud wail, which,
being interpreted, means "give me food." Where will he get it?
He will get it from the earth—by whatever devious process it is
refined. That little body-mind must be nourished and everything
it takes to feed him, clothe him, shelter him, warm him—tons
and tons of it, will have to come out of the earth. There is nothing
here to feed upon except the earth—what it contains, what it
produces, the everlasting miracle of the good earth. The earth
is a great pantry which nature has been storing up for millions
of years, and every person who comes to live in this world lives
off it and takes something out of it.

About a hundred and fifty years ago people began to be disturbed about that—the twin problems of population and produc-
tion. A gloomy Englishman named Malthus wrote a book that
frightened men out of their wits. He predicted that the world
was gradually moving toward global famine—the world was producing people faster than it was producing material to support
them. He wanted to see population checked because there was
only a certain amount in nature's pantry. With the population
going up and the food supply going down, the day was coming
when there would not be enough. That frightened people, and
set going a land-grabbing spree of colonial expansion. Later
scientists disproved his conclusions and his premise. They said he
did not have the facts right, and he did not have the right facts;
that he had vastly underestimated the world's resources and
man's resourcefulness. Since then many things have happened to
quiet the fear—the opening up of new continents, mass produc-
tion techniques, refrigeration of food, many other things which
Malthus did not see nor foresee.

But today that old theory is coming back; the ghost of Malthus
walks again; the specter of overpopulation and underproduction
is beginning again to haunt us, and questions about the world's

waste and the world's want are very much in our minds and in our problems.

Who looks for the rules of economics in religion? Who would have thought that the world's basic problem of bread would be foreshadowed in a parable of Jesus? A boy who wasted his substance came to want because he was not worthy of his heritage. Could you get it in a smaller capsule than that? How one would like to walk into the hospitals and homes where these new arrivals have come, sit down by their cots, and against the background of a great parable, talk straight to them about the world into which they have come and what they must do to live worthily in it. Let us talk to them loudly enough for all to hear.

I suppose the first thing we would say to them is that they must learn to work. Work is definitely a part of the divine plan for life. God created everything but He manufactures nothing. Our very existence on this planet involves us in a *partnership* in which we take the raw material which God has so bountifully provided and by the application of intelligence and energy, transform it into bread, buildings, substance suitable to our use. We call that energy "work."

We can't escape that partnership. There is no bread without work, somebody's. God has ordained as a basic law of life that man shall earn his bread by the sweat of his brow, pay his way, put something in for what he takes out. And if he tries to live by unearned bread, if he makes no return of brain or brawn for what he takes out, he will sin against his nature and demoralize his soul.

The first mark of the prodigal mind is the idea that one can be a gentleman, live in the world without work or on the labor of others. "Give me the goods," the boy said to his father, and went off down the road to spend what somebody else had worked for. He ceased to be a worker and became a waster, a user, not a producer. That's what the word "prodigal" means—waster.

And it is not surprising that there came a day when he began to be in want, for these two things go together—waste and want, idleness and emptiness. When people take from the table of life without putting anything back, they become the kind of people who create want and famine in the earth.

So the first thing we would say to those new arrivals—you are in a partnership—if you don't propose to work here you'd better get your robe on and migrate to Mars—you've landed on the wrong planet. This is a work world and all who live in it must make some return for the space they occupy and for what they take from the table of the earth.

More than that, they must learn to worship, bow themselves down before the Giver of life, live in appreciation of the gift. Our very existence here involves us in a *stewardship* as well as a partnership. We do not own the earth, nor any part of it. Maybe six feet of it some time. The earth is indeed the Lord's. The world is literally the Father's house, and if we will not live in appreciation of this heritage, conserve the resources of the earth, we shall someday come to want in it.

We can never forget the story of the first man, set down in a garden to keep it, care for it, live off the fruits of it, develop his life upon it. And when he sinned against the nature of the garden and the purpose of the Gardener, something in the land struck back in thorns and thistles. Adam lost his garden and got a wilderness. That isn't myth. That is the true story of man from Adam on, living here in this planet garden, not as a good steward of its resources but more like a spendthrift prodigal who, having received a heritage from his father, proceeded to throw it carelessly away. You can trace that story in today's conflicts. Trouble in Africa—black and white. Read *Cry, the Beloved Country* in which Alan Paton describes the congestion of native Africans in white cities because "the land won't keep them any more." Trouble in Asia—Arab and Jew; lands which in Bible times were rich, supporting millions of people and thriving cities, through centuries of misuse lost their fertility until people moved out of them leaving dead cities and desert vastness because "the land won't keep them any more."

Some angry books are being written now about this new world and the waste of the past three hundred years. When the white men came here they found a continent rich in natural resources, virgin forests, grass lands, lakes and rivers teeming with fish, forests abounding in wild game. "A new Garden of Eden," someone called it. They moved in from the Atlantic coast line, these hardy sons of the Old World, swarmed down into the lush valleys, cutting down and burning up the timber as they came. Lumber, they called it (a word which originally meant trash). Lumber— trees, only God can make them. Any fool can destroy them, and we've been doing that with irresponsible prodigality until the Forestry Service warns us that we're only a few years away from the bottom of the woodpile, hardly any virgin timber left. They plowed up lands that should not have been plowed, overgrazed the grass lands, slaughtered the animals for nothing but their hides. Then one day the sun was darkened with dust storms and the starved earth struck back in the undernourished people on Tobacco Road, and the oakies wandering about because "the land won't keep them any more."

What has happened to the sparkling waters of our lakes and rivers? Tons of refuse dumped in them, sewerage from cities, waste products from mills and factories, until almost every major city is having water trouble. It is the old story of Adam turning a garden into a wilderness. These alarming books which have been written tell us we have now reached the point where unless our wastefulness stops, that our sin against the land can wipe us out as effectively as atomic fire.

Fortunately there is a hopeful other side to the picture, some evidence that the downward trend is now being reversed. Con-

servation is a word which has been in our national vocabulary
only forty years. For example, in the year I was born my father
was breaking his back with a stumping machine, rooting out the
trees to make a farm. Today within half a century, my brother-
in-law, living on the same farm, is also a member of Parliament
in the Ontario House, and the government has put him on the
Conservation Commission whose duty it is to put back the trees
and replenish the forests of Ontario. That is a parable. The last
generation destroyed the trees to make a living. This generation
is learning to put them back. We are learning also to put something back into the soil. All through the world men are becoming
conservation conscious, putting back the trees, bringing back the
land, and through fear and necessity learning to be better
stewards of the land.

So the second thing we would say to these new arrivals, and
to ourselves—you must learn stewardship—if you keep the land
the land will keep you—if you waste the land you and your
descendants will come to want in it.

Then we must say to them a final and more urgent word. If
they are to live worthily here they must learn to love, indeed if
they are to live at all. By the very nature of our existence, we're
involved in a *fellowship,* linked by a thousand invisible bonds
with other people, millions of them whom we must learn to love
and live with or collectively destroy the earth in suicidal strife.
Would it not be startling to these newly arrived citizens if someone could break the news to them that every baby born here in
America starts life owing eighteen hundred dollars, his per capita
share of the national debt? Perhaps that partly explains the rising
birth rate. Apparently these babies have made up their minds
that if this generation is to pay the war debt, there had better be
a lot of them. Two hundred and seventy-five billion dollars!
Maybe they should learn to love. The cost of hate comes high.

This has been the most destructive, wasteful half century in human history. Unable to live in peace with one another, we have squandered our substance with riotous abandon. We went down into the mines, dug their precious metal, hurled great chunks of it at one another. To preserve our oil, we have burned up tons of it, enough to keep our tractors going for a hundred years. To defend our homes, we have demolished homes, millions of homes in Europe and Asia, shattered our cities, scattered their people on the roads, homeless and hungry—thirty million refugees. How long can the good earth stand the cost of hate? How long can the oil last, the copper and the timber? How far is it to famine in the far country of ill will? Maybe we had better learn to love. The price of hate comes high.

This is no time, of course, for glib language. No one is naïve enough to think that in this sort of world we can lay down our arms. But what troubles us beyond words to express is the terrific disproportion between what we are willing to do in one direction and what we are failing to do in the direction that matters most. How far would the appeal of communism go if out in the areas where it gets its converts it had to compete with a democracy that had learned to love and conquer the world by serving it, as Jesus said?

That cost of hate is getting higher. A United States senator figured out what it costs to kill an enemy soldier. In Caesar's war you could get a good enemy corpse for about seventy-five cents. In Napoleon's war the price went up to three thousand dollars. In the Civil War, five thousand; in World War I, twenty thousand; in World War II, fifty thousand. Other statisticians looking at the whole show, taking the total cost and the total killed in all lands, figured that now it costs the world a million and a half to kill one man. How far is it to famine? We are beginning to feel the pinch of it. Having wasted our substance in unworthy living, we are beginning to feel the want—in diminishing commodities, in the piling up of war debts, in higher and higher taxes. Maybe that's our hope. When people feel the pinch in their pocketbooks they begin to ponder. That's what happened to the prodigal. There came a great day for him. He began to be in want. He began to think straight. He came to himself. "What am I doing here?" he asked. "In my father's house there is enough and to spare. Why should I be in want?"

There are two kinds of poverty—natural and artificial—and it finally dawned on him that his hunger was wholly artificial, self made. He was living in a famine which his own folly had produced. It simply did not need to be. "In my father's house there is enough and to spare."

Do you know that in 1944 Kirtley F. Mather, a geologist of Harvard, wrote a book on economics with that as its title— *Enough and To Spare*? The theme of his book was precisely this, that famine in the modern world is almost wholly unnecessary. For the first time in history man possesses the resources and the know-how to banish famine and provide all mankind with the necessities of life. This is not a burned-out planet, as some bright folks tell us. There are no bottlenecks in providence. There is no failure in the good earth. To be sure, there are floods and droughts and land erosions which once were resigned to as acts of God, but most floods can be controlled. Swamp lands can be reclaimed, deserts can be irrigated, even topsoil can be replaced. Soil men are enthusiastic about what can be done now to replenish the soil. There is no lack of land. Twenty-five million square miles of it tillable of which we are using less than seven million and much of that not well.

A new light has come into man's mind in recent years which we believe is the light of God. God has been good to our age in giving us knowledge of vitamins, nutrition, the chemistry of food and what someone calls "the versatility of molecules." In this suit I am wearing today there is not a stitch of wool or cotton. It is made out of air and water and a little coal. In Florida within the past twenty years we have had an agricultural revolution. With the introduction of new grasses, new breeds of cattle, the fertilization of pastures, the eradication of the tick, Florida has become the second largest pasture cattle-producing state east of the Mississippi. Look out, Texas, here we come!

Conservationists believe that with the new light on agriculture we have added to the earth the equivalent of another continent. It is literally true that in our Father's house there is enough and to spare, provided we live worthily.

Stanley Jones, speaking on the prodigal, said when he decided to go home and co-operate with his father, the father threw open everything he had to him—the fatted calf, the best robe, shoes for his feet, the father's house. Food, shelter, clothing, everything the father possessed was his when he decided to be a son. It sets you thinking what would happen in this world if we learned to love and live as sons. "It is your Father's good pleasure," said Jesus, "to give you the kingdom." What then are we waiting for? Technically the bread problem is already solved. We have the skill if we had the will. What is needed is a new spirit, a new birth, a new life in Christ through which we learn to love; to be born from above, through the atoning work of Christ and the reconciling power of his holy spirit.

Our missionaries have been showing the way. With the very little they've had to work with they have performed miracles and shown us how we can conquer the world by loving it. Dr. Sam Higginbottom, on his farm in India, has demonstrated over the past four decades that if the people are poor it is not because the land is poor. With the use of fertilizer, better breeding of cattle, improved methods of agriculture, the land is rich enough to feed the hungry hordes and have enough left over for the sacred cows. It is not a matter of giving people our resources. It is more a matter of assisting them under God to develop to the utmost the resources they possess. That requires love. When do we start? When do we start dedicating the great money power of American churches to the basic needs of life?

# 7

## Christianity and Health

### By E. STANLEY JONES

CHRISTIANITY IS NOT A HEALING CULT. ITS CENTRAL PURPOSE IS not to keep the body in repair. God is not a cosmic bellhop we can call in to attend to our needs. If we undertake to *use* God, we'll *lose* God. So God is not here just to keep us well, nor is He here to make us merely happy. There are those who would use Christianity as a happiness cult. They're calling on God to help them out of depression and moods, largely the result of their own wrong actions.

But while Christianity is not a healing cult and its primary purpose is not to keep us in physical repair, nevertheless a part of that redemption is essentially and fundamentally moral and spiritual. Redemption of the body is largely a by-product of redemption of the soul. Jesus healed, but he asked them to keep it silent. The central thing for which he came was to redeem men from sin and evil. While that is true, nevertheless there is no force in the world that does so much to tone up the body, to make it rhythmical and harmonious, adjusted and disease free, as the Christian faith.

*E. Stanley Jones is recognized throughout the world as one of today's greatest Christian evangelists. He divides his ministery between India and America.*

71

Dr. William Samuel Sadler, the great psychiatrist, said if we lived in a truly Christian way, one-half of our diseases would drop off tomorrow morning. The only faith that I know of that takes material matter seriously is the Christian faith. It's the most materialistic of all religions. God looked upon the *earth* and saw that it was good. The material was God-created, God-approved. And the central idea of the Christian faith is the Incarnation— God's redemptive invasion of us, the Divine Word become *flesh*. The material was not to be alien, it was to be a part, an agent of redemption. Therefore, *God wills health*. He's come to redeem the total person and total society from everything that's destructive and especially that most destructive thing called evil—sin. Therefore disease is never the will of God. God no more wills disease of the body than he wills disease of the soul. The Lambeth Conference said: "However disease may be brought about and in whatever way it may be overruled for good, it is in itself an evil." The evil of the mind is error, the evil of the emotion is suffering, the evil of the body is disease, the evil of the soul is sin.

And so Jesus came to launch a redemptive movement, to redeem us from every evil including the evil called disease. When Jesus announced the Kingdom of God, he said to his disciples, "Go out and say, 'The kingdom of God is at hand, heal the sick.'" A part of the redemptive impact of the Kingdom of God upon the framework of human nature was the healing of the sick.

Now, this redeeming of the body is seen in the light of modern medical findings. Modern medical science says that some diseases are structural while others are functional; some are rooted in the body and some are rooted in the mind and the spirit. The American Medical Association says it's about fifty-fifty—about 50 per cent of the diseases are rooted in wrong mental and spiritual attitudes and about 50 per cent are rooted in physical causes. Sometimes the body gets sick and passes on its sicknesses to the mind and to the soul. And sometimes the mind and the soul get sick and pass on their sicknesses to the body. And the doctors are ready to say that it's about fifty-fifty. I said that one day to a medical man, a doctor, and he said, "Fifty-fifty nothing—75 per cent of the people who come to me don't need medicine." They were passing on the sicknesses of their minds and of their souls to their bodies and they won't be well until they change their attitudes toward life.

Professor James says, "The greatest revolution in my generation was the discovery that human beings can alter the outer aspects of their lives by changing their inner attitudes of mind. A great many of our *outer* aspects of life can be changed, if we change our *inner* attitudes. There was a time when we handed over the body to the doctor, the mind to the educator and the psychiatrist and the soul to the minister, and we said, "Take care of each." Now we know that that can't be done. Man is a unit and has to be treated as a unit. A man from the Mayo Clinic said to me, "We can deal with 25 per cent of the people who come to us with the instruments of science, but we don't know what to do with the 75 per cent." You can't reach their sicknesses by the instruments of science. Their illnesses come out of mental and spiritual attitudes.

We also know now that not one single cell of the body is completely removed from the effects of mind and emotion. In the Battle Creek Sanatorium, an experiment was carried on with a dog, a friendly little fellow. After an operation it was found that in the marrow of his bones, the red corpuscles were there in abundance. He was in a very healthy state. The wound from the operation healed quickly. Then word was passed down the line that no one was to pay any attention to the dog. He was to be left severely alone. The dog was puzzled, hurt, and then would hide away under the furniture in grief. In that state of mind, they operated on him again and they discovered that the marrow of his bones was almost free from red corpuscles, a dark brownish color, and the incision healed very slowly. But finally the dog got well. Then they asked everybody to pay attention to the dog and be friendly. The dog refused to respond at first, but then he began to be friendly again himself. He was his own joyous, bounding self. In that state of mind they operated on him again and they discovered that the red corpuscles, in the marrow of his bones, were in a normal state. And the incision healed quickly.

What had happened? The effect of the emotions of grief, sorrow, disappointment, frustration had gone down to the marrow of his bones. So, when you say "I feel it in my *bones*," you're right. You *do* feel it in your bones, for the effect of mind and emotion reaches clear down to the marrow of your bones. An emotion, somebody has said, is a change in the mind which produces a sensible change in the body.

There was a man who was allergic to roses; he got asthma every time he got near roses. Once he was handed some paper roses and he got an attack. I once heard of another man who had asthma every day at five o'clock. One day he woke up at seven o'clock and realized that he had not had an attack. Forthwith he had one. A woman said to me, "I have anticipatory asthma. I anticipate it and become frightened and get an attack."

Now, don't misunderstand me. I don't say that all diseases are mentally and spiritually produced. There are diseases of the tissues and they are real. And there are contagious diseases and they are real. But a great many of our diseases are rooted in the mental and spiritual. For instance, here was a soldier completely paralyzed. Because of the conflict in his desire between doing his duty and a desire to run away, he produced a paralysis as a way out. Here was a woman who didn't like to be a pastor's wife and she produced a paralysis and became an invalid. Her husband and the congregation waited on her. Then the husband died and she got up from her bed and stumped the state for the Republican party. She had produced a paralysis to get out of a situation she didn't like.

Now, what are we to do about this whole matter? First of all, *talk health to yourself, not disease*. You say, "That's autosuggestion." Of course it is. But don't go around talking about how ill you are. If you do, you'll be more ill. And don't go around talking about how tired you are. If you do, you'll be more tired. The Japanese have a saying of sympathy, "You must be tired." I heard it everywhere: "You must be tired." And my invariable answer was, "Well, if I should say I am tired, I would be more tired, so I don't say I am tired, I say, I am fresh in God." Not in myself, but in God and in His resources. When I can take His resources, then I am fresh.

Second, *give up all fears*. I asked a doctor, "Is fear enemy number one?" He replied, "It's enemy number one and a half." He said there's nothing so terrible as allowing fear in your life. Freud found the source of neurosis in the past, in childhood. Jung found it in the present. He says, "I no longer find the source of neurosis in the past, but in the present. What is the necessary task which the patient will not accomplish, what's he afraid of, what's he running away from? What's the responsibility that he is refusing to take up?"

A man said to me one day, "Will you autograph this book? I want to send it to a hotelkeeper, a Roman Catholic." I said, "That's interesting. Why?" "Well," he said, "I had ulcers, couldn't get any insurance. I was sick and afraid. And this Roman Catholic hotelkeeper handed me your book, *The Way*." He said, "I began to read it. I was full of fears. I surrendered my fears into the hands of God. He took them over and made me over." And he added, "My stomach ulcers cleared up. I couldn't get any insurance before, now I've got $35,000."

Then, *give up all resentments*. Resentments are poison. A doctor told me one day of a man who hadn't worked for ten years because of high blood pressure and a bad heart. He said, "I turned to him and I asked, 'Against whom are you holding a resentment?' The man looked at me in surprise and said, 'Well, I've got a grudge against my nephew.' " And the doctor said, "You and I had better go to that nephew." They went and sat down together. They buried this resentment, came back and the man's blood pressure came down. His heart ceased to act up. A few days later he was back at his work.

Dr. Alvarez tells of a man who came to the Mayo Clinic who couldn't think of a thing except the fact that his sister had brought a law suit against him. He chewed on that, night and day. His breath became foul. Every organ became affected. In six months he was dead. He was killed by the poison of resentments. A man felt that he was allergic to the fur coat which his mother-in-law wore. Every time that he would get near her, he would have an attack of asthma. And then one day, she wore another coat and he got another attack. Then one day talking to her over the telephone, he got another attack. It wasn't an allergy. Just simple resentment. A doctor said to me one day, "I couldn't find any physical basis for a woman's vomiting until one day she incidentally said that her mother-in-law was coming to visit her at Thanksgiving. I called the husband and I said to him, "Do you want your wife to be well?" And he replied, "I certainly do." Then the doctor said, "You send a telegram to your mother suggesting that she postpone her visit." The telegram was sent off, word was brought to the wife that the mother-in-law was not coming. The vomiting stopped. When you say, "He makes me *sick*," that's right. Or you say, "He's a *pain* in the neck," you are right. When you say, "Oh, that woman's a headache," you're right. You react in anger, resentment, and you get a headache.

Fourth, *surrender all self-centeredness*. With yourself on your own hands, you have a problem and a pain. But with yourself in the hands of God, you have a possibility and a power. Adler says,

"I suppose all the ills of human personality can be traced back to one thing—not understanding the meaning of the phrase 'It is more blessed to give than to receive.' " You've got to get yourself off your own hands. Therefore, self-surrender is essential.

My fifth suggestion is that *you make peace with your conscience*. A businessman went to a doctor because he couldn't sleep and was nervously upset. The doctor asked, "Is there something on your conscience?" "Doctor," he replied, "I came here not to be pried into, but to be treated medically." And he went away in a huff. The next day he returned. "Doctor," he said, "there is something on my conscience. There was an inheritance and I stole my brother's share." The doctor replied, "Sit down and write that to your brother." He obeyed. After the letter was written, the doctor said, "I'll go with you to mail it." He knew how hard it would be to mail that letter. But the businessman replied, "Oh, no, you've got lots of patients here, I'll go and mail it." "No," said the doctor, "I'll sneak out the back way and they won't know I'm gone." So they stole out the back way, went across the street, and when the letter hit the bottom of the box, he grabbed the doctor's hand and he said, "Doctor, I am well." And he was. The guilt functioned as a disturbance in his system and he would never be a well man until he got that guilt out. No wonder the head of a medical college said to me one day, "If you ministers can't produce conversion, we doctors will have to for life demands it."

Now, some general suggestions: first, *self-surrender is absolutely necessary*. You've got to lose your life to find it. A psychiatrist has written a pamphlet on the therapeutic value of self-surrender. What we ministers have long been talking about, namely, self-surrender, is now confirmed by psychology. You've got to lose your life. God's *God*, not *you*, and if you organize life around yourself, life won't approve of you. So when Jesus said, "He that saveth his life shall lose it, and he that loseth it shall find it," he put his finger on the center of our problem—self-surrender.

Then, *keep the Quiet Time.* In the pure strong hours of the morning, when the soul of the day is at its best, lean upon the window sill of God and look into His face and get the orders for the day. Then go out into the day with the sense of a Hand on your shoulder. A *hand* on your shoulder and not a *chip*—a sense of mission and commission! If you have that quiet hour in the morning, you will have the quiet heart through the day and you will come to the night with a quiet heart.

Next, *don't try to regulate the body too much.* It is made for health. If you spend too much time at it, you'll upset the functions of the body. I know of a man who had a slight difficulty with his knee. It frightened him and his wife and they spent the balance of their days attending to that knee. They gave it attention pains. Obey the laws of health and get interested in somebody else and let your troubles alone. Somebody asked Dr. Menninger, the great psychiatrist, "Suppose a nervous breakdown is imminent, what are you to do?" That great psychiatrist suggested a very simple thing: "Turn the key in your door. Walk out across the tracks, find some people who need you and do something for them. And you'll probably ward off a nervous breakdown." Get interested in something beyond yourself.

Remember, *receptivity is the way to live.* Learn how to receive. Joy is the best medicine. Outgoing love tones up the system. Think positive, not negative thoughts. I have a friend who takes hold of sick personalities and the first thing he does with them is to make them say "yes" twenty-five times. They had been saying "No, no, no. I can't do this. I won't do that. I won't do the other." And he makes them sit down and say "yes, yes, yes" twenty-five times to get them started on a positive way to live.

*God heals in a number of ways,* not one. First through the physician and the surgeon. The physician and the surgeon do not heal, they simply clear the way for the healing forces which are resident there and have been put there by God. They heal. *The doctor tends us, but God heals.* The doctor can only clear the way for the health-giving forces which are resident to assert themselves and bring you to health. So God heals *through* the physician and the surgeon. And I am grateful.

*God also heals through climate and through mental suggestion.* You can suggest health or you can suggest sickness. He also heals by delivering us from underlying fears, worries, anxieties, self-centeredness and guilts which produce disease.

God also heals directly with his touch upon our bodies. I know. Thirty-six years ago I was a broken man. They told me that if I went on at that pace in India I would break within a year, but I managed to stick it out for eight-and-a-half and then I had a nervous break. I took a year's furlough and came back to America to regain my shattered health. On my way back to India I saw that I was far from well. While holding meetings in the Philippine Islands, the same collapses came back. I went on to India with a deepening cloud upon me. Here I was beginning a new term of service, but broken. All the time I felt called to do the kind of work that I have been doing since, but I was unfit mentally, spiritually, physically. I went to the mountains on arrival, took some months off.

The last time I came down I saw that the game was up. I'd have to give up my mission work and the ministry in order to regain my shattered health. It was a dark hour. I was in the back of a church at Lucknow, not praying for myself particularly, but in prayer when the Inner Voice said to me, "Are you yourself ready for this work to which I have called you?" I said, "No. I am done for. I have reached the end of my resources and can't go on." And He said to me, "If you will turn it over to me and not worry about it, I'll take care of it." I remember my eager reply, "Lord, I close the bargain right here." I rose from my knees knowing I was a well man. I scarcely touched the earth as I walked home that night, so lifted up was I in soul and in body.

For days after that when nightfall would come, I wondered why in the world I should ever go to bed. There wasn't the slightest trace of tiredeness of any kind. I wondered if I should tell this and felt that I should, and did publicly. It scared my friends. They were afraid it wouldn't work and so when they would meet me, they'd say, "Stanley, how are you?" It's been thirty-six years ago. It's never returned. And I've become strongest in the place where I was weakest, namely, in nervous energy. I've been speaking from three to five times a day for these thirty-six years. When I come to the end of a day I can hold out my hand and it's quite steady. In other words, I've become strongest at the place where I was weakest. But I know it was the gift of God and I must watch my margins. He can and does heal us directly.

Then *there is the final healing in the Resurrection.* Some diseases may have to wait that final cure. Paul had one, a thorn in the flesh. He asked God to take it away and he said, "No, my grace is sufficient for you." Then Paul said, "I glory in my infirmities." God will either heal the disease, or give you power to use the infirmity until the final cure in the Resurrection. A friend of mine, an evangelist, who was a good singer, was stricken in the vocal cords by—of all things—cancer. The whole voice box had to be removed, so he had no way to speak. A slit was made in his throat and he breathed through that slit. Then he said to himself, "If I can't talk, I'll learn to play a violin." He learned to play a violin at sixty-five. Then he said, "They tell me that maybe I can speak without vocal cords." And he began to speak without vocal cords, swallowing the air down into his stomach and then bringing it back and making words with his tongue and the roof of his mouth. He could carry on a conversation without vocal cords. And he said eagerly, "You know, I can already speak over the microphone to an audience and some of these days I am going to speak to a big audience."

No, disease is not the will of God, He is out to cure it. And if we will surrender ourselves to Him, he'll either cure us of our diseases, or give us power to use them until the final cure in the Resurrection.

# 8

# God's Good News

## By GERALD KENNEDY

ONE OF THE GREAT LEADERS OF OUR CHURCH OF THE LAST
century was Bishop William Taylor. In the beginning of his
ministry he was a missionary to California. I follow in his train.
He went out there in the days of '49 and came to San Francisco.
There he discovered that there was no church for him to preach
in, and not very many people anxious to hear him preach, but he
noticed that on Sunday morning on the streets of the city there
were vast crowds of people, mostly men, so on Sunday morning
he would take a barrel and roll it down to a street corner, stand
up on top of it and raise a great shout, "What's the news?"
When they gathered around to hear what this strange fellow had
to say, he would begin his preaching by saying, "Thank God, my
brethren, I have good news for you this morning."

We must never forget that the Gospel means "good news," and
we who preach it ought to so declare it, and we who hear it ought
to be ready to hear something exciting, something very startling.
We are not to think of the Gospel as a book of home remedies.
On the contrary it is headline stuff, somebody yelling "Extra!
Something has happened! Something tremendous! Better stop

*Gerald Kennedy is bishop of the Los Angeles area of the Meth-
odist Church.*

and hear what it is!" Tonight I want for a little while therefore to talk to you about the Gospel as the "good news," and I want to say three or four things.

First this: The Gospel is the good news of *personality*. It is the good news that at the heart and center of the universe there is a person—that God is a person. One of our great mistakes in our time is to confuse the Gospel with a particular system. We want to make it the same thing as a political system, or an economic system. So that sometimes it comes out like this: a man will say, "After all, Christianity is democracy." So far, so good. That's a general statement. Nobody argues. The next step is, "Christianity is American democracy," and if you say it in America, most people will agree with that. The next step is to say that Christianity is the Republican party's interpretation of American democracy—or the Democratic party's, wherever you happen to be. And according to where you are, that will be accepted. Then you go one step further and you say, "Christianity is either the Eisenhower or the McCarthy side of the Republican party's interpretation of democracy," and that's bad, because it isn't true. And finally you come to the place where you're saying that Christianity is nothing more nor less than my favorite political idea, or my economic insight. That's my religion. We must never forget that the Gospel has to be proclaimed and demonstrated in all kinds of society. It comes as a shock to many people that behind the Iron Curtain there are millions of witnessing Christians, that even in Russia there is a church. As far ahead as we can see, the Church will have to function in all kinds of societies. We must never get so narrow as to believe that Christianity is merely this or that system.

Now this doesn't mean that the Gospel has no concern with systems. It has. But it always comes to ask of every political or economic system certain questions, the real questions. It's most important to know the right questions. A man was going down the street one day, saw a little boy looking after a baby, stopped, and he asked, "Son, what is your little brother's name?" The little boy looked up and said, "If he was my brother his name might be Jack but she ain't, and her name is Ruth." You ask the wrong questions and you get the wrong answers. So the Gospel comes to ask of every system the right questions. It comes to say, "What happens to people in this organization? What is the status of women? What happens to children? What happens to the aged, to the sick, to the infirm? What happens to persons?" That is the ultimate question asked of any system. And the good news of the Gospel is this, that any system which does not have persons at the heart and center of its values is a system that is doomed. The universe, the stars, fight on the side of personality, and the measure at the end of the day of the strength of a nation is what happens to people within the confines of that nation.

We should not forget—we in America or anywhere else, but especially here in America now—those words spoken in that famous essay on "Liberty" by John Stuart Mill. He said, "A nation that dwarfs its men that they may become more docile instruments for its purposes will discover that with small men no great thing can be accomplished." And the purpose of any society is to create big men, great men, for that's the measure of its strength, that's the measure of its future. And this is good news, the good news of persons.

In the second place, the Gospel comes to tell us the good news of *joy*. This is rather a startling thing for some people to hear, that religion is supposed to be fun. I have said sometimes on a college campus that I'm a Christian, partly because I think it's more fun being a Christian than anything else I know about. That is a most amazing thing! You can see by the expression on the faces of the students that it never dawned on them that Christianity is joy. Read your New Testament. One of its minor miracles is that so many people who apparently had no cause for happiness found that when they met Jesus a new joy, an absurd kind of happiness, took hold of them in the most untoward circumstances. There was Jesus himself. "The foxes have holes, the birds of the air have nests, but the Son of Man hath not where to lay his head." Homeless, wandering around, certain after a while that he was heading toward a great trouble, and death, yet there's a strange joy about him, constantly. Little children come to him. People must have smiled when he preached. There are things in the Gospel which, if we had not heard them so often, would still strike us as humorous. There's a wonderful verse in the Book of Hebrews. That unknown author writes, speaking of our Lord, "Who, for the joy that was set before him, endured the cross," as if even this could not take from him the sense of joy of conquest.

Or turn to the Apostle Paul. There's a man who had very little to make him happy, we should say. Well, let me read it. You find that he recounts something of his life when he writes to the Corinthians. In the second letter that he wrote to the Corinthians he says, "Five times I have received at the hands of the Jews the forty lashes less one. Three times I have been beaten with rods; once I was stoned. Three times I have been shipwrecked; a night and a day I have been adrift at sea; on frequent journeys, in danger from rivers, danger from robbers, danger from my own people, danger from Gentiles, danger in the city, danger in the wilderness, danger at sea, danger from false brethren; in toil and hardship, through many a sleepless night, in hunger and thirst, often without food, in cold and exposure. And apart from other things, there is the daily pressure upon me of my anxiety for the churches" (r.s.v.) Does that sound like the diary of a happy man? Well, it is. Strange thing, isn't it? You can hardly read anywhere in Paul's letters but that he does not break forth with this thing. He says to the Philippians: "Rejoice! And again I will say unto you, Rejoice!" This was the man who could be writing about a church quarrel and suddenly break into the most wonderful poem on "Love" the world ever saw. Read the 13th Chapter of I Corinthians. Everything against it, and yet oddly enough this strange man finding happiness, joy unspeakable, full of glory.

And to some extent that was true of all those early Christians. There was so little in their lives to make them happy. There was no social status to be gained by joining the First Methodist Church of Jerusalem. Quite the opposite. It meant that when they joined that group, they met danger. No good business contacts to be made in that congregation, and nobody was rich, and nobody was successful. Paul talks about that too. He says most of them were poor, most of them were unknown. Yet these are the ones, with a quality in them which made them exciting. "This is the man they say is coming to us. He's upsetting the world." "Behold," said those pagans, "how these Christians love one another." And there was a happiness within them.

Maybe we're on the wrong track. Maybe the things we think are necessary for happiness aren't the real things after all. Maybe we had better read again the experience of those first-century Christians who were close to Christ, who had the experience fresh in their hearts. Ah, there's something about that, something wonderful, a sense of victory. And you can always tell that a real Christian has been close to his Lord because he's full of this joy. "Let all the world and every corner sing, My God and King!"

And I am convinced that the people who have the best time in the world are preachers. You feel sorry for them. You don't need to. They feel sorry for you. And the best stories I ever hear are at the Council of Bishops. You won't believe that but that's true. Christians have more fun than anyone else, and it's because somehow they know that life makes sense. The war isn't over but the decisive battle has been won. It was won at Calvary on Good Friday. And because they know that their life makes sense and there's dignity in it, and value, no matter what comes

along there bursts forth from them this sense, this wonderful
sense of joy.

Some years ago Charles Eliot of Harvard went to Europe and
went to church in London. He wrote home to his son about the
experience. He said, "Yesterday we attended M——'s church,
heard an excellent sermon, badly delivered. The whole service
lacked cheerfulness. The tones of M——'s voice and his reflec-
tions were all depressing. It is almost the worst of faults in a
preacher. Faith, hope and love are all cheerful things and ought
to be made to appear so by those who preach them. Life is not
always bright, but religion should be." It should be. It was
Claudel, the French poet, who said that after he had heard
Beethoven's "Fifth Symphony" he knew that at the heart of the
universe there is joy. How much more then that man who has
been found by God in Christ knows that at the heart of the universe there is joy! The good news which I am called upon to
proclaim, and every Christian is, is the good news of joy.

Now the third thing that ought to be said, it seems to me, is
that we proclaim also the good news of *freedom*. We don't make
enough of this. The man who has been found by God is the man
who has been set free. He has been set free from his own frustrations, his anxieties and his fears, from his narrowness, his bitterness, his dogmatism. I do not know anything more contradictory
than a Christian who is mean because he is self-consciously ortho-
dox, and he thinks that everyone who disagrees with him ought
to be persecuted. We sometimes think of freedom—and this is a
mistake of our day—as an extracurricular activity of life—you
take it or you leave it, some people want it, some don't, make your
choice. It's no such thing. God wills that men should be free.
Men *must* be free, for without freedom there is no culture, and
there is no achievement of personal destiny. I have seen enough
evidence, for example, to convince me that one of the reasons the
Nazis lost the war was the fact that they put around their scientists

fear, regimentation, suspicion and distrust. At the end of the day, if a nation has no higher motive than security, no higher motive than to exist, let that nation stay free. Let its citizens be free, for without freedom a nation goes down.

The so-called literature which the Communists are now producing in Russia is not really literature at all. It's so much propaganda. Ah, how the mighty have fallen! The people that produced the great Russian novelists of the nineteenth century producing the stuff that comes out of there now! Because a man can't write a great book when he's not free. The Russian art is second rate, and the poetry does not sing. When you have to have your eye upon the Kremlin and ask what is pleasing to the party leaders, you produce no art that is worthy of the name. If you are to have a civilized life, a cultured life, if you are to produce the thing which will not die, then you must have freedom. You do not produce greatness when you have teachers who are frightened to death that sooner or later they will be subject to some kind of persecution from an investigating committee, and that if by chance they've said anything which can be twisted around as being outside the party line, whatever it may be at that time, they will be discharged. America depends upon its public school system. Let us have teachers who are first rate, as they have been. You cannot drive people like that out of the school system and have a future. You cannot frighten people so they'll deal only with dead issues and have a future. We grew up on controversy. We believe that men will choose the truth. Let them know the truth, and let that man who may be a heretic have freedom for his heresy, and don't call him subversive.

It is very, very important that every man should believe that the pulpit of the nation is free. Alexis de Tocqueville, one of the great students of America, and a man who understood it as well as any outsider ever understood it, I think, said that one of the main strengths of America is her free pulpits preaching righteous-

ness. Let the clergy be free men. And I believe with all my heart
they will be, because they must be. We betray our commission
when we are silent when we should speak, when the prophetic
note is gone. This is not something we have a choice about. It is
something we must do, because God has given us a word to speak,
and it is a word of freedom. This is good news. It's good news to
everybody except the tyrants, that because we are the sons of God
we were made for liberty. Ultimately, finally, that system which
denies liberty will go down, because God made us free. We were
born free. It is our heritage.

You remember the Dreyfus affair. A reactionary military regime in France had made a scapegoat out of a Jewish officer and
sent him away to Devil's Island. They thought it was a closed
case because the law said that once it had been adjudicated it
could not be raised again. It was done. It was finished. The lid
was on it. Then came Zola, who wrote that wonderful essay,
*J'accuse,* and was brought to trial because he was raising something that was supposed to be kept quiet, that was ended. You
may remember in the story of that famous trial that when his
lawyer came to the end and was summing up, he pointed to a
crucifix which hung on the wall just above the judge's head and
he said, "They said that case was closed too." Because you could
not close that case, because after Good Friday comes Easter morning, we have before us this assurance, this living parable, that you
never close the case on men's freedom. And that's good news.

The last thing I should like to say this evening is that our Gospel
is the good news of *power*. I read a good many books these days
telling us how to be happy. They don't help me much, because
they're saying essentially, so many of them, the way to be happy
is to adjust yourself to the way things are. We've made a cult out
of adjustment. You find out what you have to do and you adjust
your life to it, so, all comes out well. Does it really? You know,
during the war, in some of the occupied countries, there were

people who took that philosophy and said, "The enemy is here. We might as well trade with him. We can do him some service and he will do some service for us. We have to live with the way things are. This is the situation. Adjust to it." The trouble was that after the enemy was driven out and the government was re-established, they called those people collaborators, and some of them were hanged.

I'm not so sure about this adjustment business. I don't believe it is the truth I need to hear. I don't believe it's the good news I'm looking for, if I know my own heart. Oh, I know as well as you do that when there's pain, the thing I want above everything else is to get rid of it. When I have a heavy load, I want first of all to get rid of it (even if you have to carry it for me). I know that if there is a duty I do not want to perform, I would like first of all to drug my conscience in such a way that I can believe that it is not my duty and I do not have to do it. But it doesn't bring me much lasting satisfaction. And finally I know that I would rather be the kind of person who can bear the pain with some courage. I would rather be the kind of person who can carry the load. I would rather be the kind of person who can do his duty. Tell me something about power to live by tonight. That's the good news I want to hear. That's the thing that speaks to my condition. Not escape. Not adjustment. But tell me where I can find the power to live nobly and heroically and joyously. That's the thing I seek and need.

You remember Paul said that he had a thorn in the flesh. We do not know what it was. Scholars have speculated. It could have been anything of a dozen different things, but it wasn't easy to bear. And he said, "I prayed three times to have it taken away and then the Lord said, 'No, I'll let you keep it but I'll give you grace enough to bear it.' " That was a more wonderful answer to Paul's prayer than anything he could have heard. It would be for me and it would be for you.

My brother-in-law came back from the war and wanted very, very much to build a house. He didn't have much money, and he found that prices were so high that they could not possibly afford to build the kind of house they wanted by having someone do it for them. And so he became his own contractor, and spent a great deal of time to get the lowest figure, and then worked himself every spare moment he had. For about a year he was at that house day and night. Finally it was finished, and I remember one night when I was up there with a mutual friend. As we sat in the living room talking that evening, this friend, looking at my brother-in-law, said, "Jim, I didn't think you could do it. I was just sure it couldn't be done. But you did it." And my brother-in-law, who is a very modest person, didn't say anything, but as I looked at him then, I saw a look of quiet satisfaction on his face, a joy deep down. He had taken a hold of something that was very, very difficult, and he had seen it through.

Ah, that's what I would like to do. That's the kind of person I would like to be. The good news which the Gospel brings to-night is not primarily the good news of peace of mind. It isn't primarily the good news that you can adjust and find some trick to manipulate things and release yourself. But it is that you shall have power—power to do what you ought to do, power to bear the load, power to persist. And that's better news, much better news than adjustment.

Some of the greatest men we've ever known have never been adjusted men. Read the prophet Jeremiah. There was a fellow who needed a counselor if there ever was one. He wasn't very happy. He says one time in his desperation that he wished he had not been born, because the job was so terrible. But he was a spiritual genius, because even in the midst of the struggle and the unhappiness and the load, he found the power to see it through. That's good news.

I close with this: Some years ago there was a mine cave-in,

and as quickly as possible a rescue party was organized because it was realized that oxygen wouldn't last very long where those men were trapped. They began to dig toward them and as they came somewhere in the vicinity they thought they heard something knocking, a tapping. They stopped and listened, and then they heard it clearly—a tapping on the rock. Those entombed men were tapping in the Morse code, "Is there any hope? Is there any hope?" And around our world tonight there are men who have been trapped by their isolation and their fear and their uncertainty, those for whom life has caved in. To every man caught in a trap like that the Gospel comes with this good news of power, and release. If only we could see it again in its freshness, if only our hearts could open again so that it might really find us, we would remember once again that the Gospel always means "good news."

# 9

# A War of Amazing Kindness

## By FRANK C. LAUBACH

YOU REMEMBER THE SCRIPTURE LESSON WHICH TELLS ABOUT
Jesus entering Jerusalem. As he came over the brow of the hill,
he saw the city. Everybody was shouting "Hosanna!" all thinking he was going in to be the king. Suddenly he burst into tears
and wept, because he knew he was not going to be king, he knew
he was going to be crucified in five days. But the thing he said—
do you remember that? It was not about himself; it was about
Jerusalem: "O, Jerusalem, if only you knew the things that
would bring you peace, but they are hidden from your eyes and
therefore there will not be one stone left upon another that will
not be torn down. Your enemies will encompass you about on
every side."

What was he talking about? Well, if you want to read a very
enlightening book, read Simkovitch's great little book, *Toward an
Understanding of Jesus,* the best book I have ever seen to explain
that amazing statement of Jesus. Simkovitch says that at that
time the Jewish nation was honeycombed with conspiracies to

*Frank C. Laubach is best known throughout the world as the
apostle to the illiterates. He serves the Committee on World
Literacy and Christian Literature, 156 Fifth Avenue, New York
10, New York.*

overthrow the Roman Empire. Jesus wanted them to conquer the Roman Empire with love, and that is what they rejected. They took the other way, the way of bloody rebellion.

How would you speak tonight if you felt what I do? As I come back from Asia and Africa, I have a message that the American people must hear right away or they will perish. That is the way I feel tonight about you. You came here perhaps to be entertained or to worship, but I came here to help save the world. And therefore I regard this as a terribly important moment, because the people who will save the world are in front of me now.

There have been two wars going on in this world today. One of them has stopped recently in Korea, but it is going on in French Indo-China. It is a hot war. We have been having a succession of those. The men who tell us how to fight such wars are in the Pentagon. They are chiefly concerned with what might happen over the North Pole. We are spending astronomical amounts of money now backing their program. The smartest military men in all America are working night and day to find a way to prevent Russia from dropping a hydrogen bomb on us. But, there is another war and that war Russia is winning through Asia and Africa at an appalling rate. It is not a possible future war, it is an enormous present war, and we are losing it.

I have just been reading the memoirs of Sir Winston Churchill which I think you all ought to read. He is telling about the Yalta Conference where he and Franklin D. Roosevelt and Joseph Stalin met. The most colossal victory in the history of mankind followed Yalta when to our utter amazement and consternation, down across China there swept a huge army and it captured China in four brief years without losing one Russian soldier! That is the greatest victory in the history of the world.

Now, the reason I'm talking about it is because the same thing is happening down through the rest of Asia and Africa now. Communists captured one-fourth of the human race without shooting a gun, at least not a Russian gun, and they are capturing another half of the human race right now. I know. There is no other American who knows any better than I do. I do not know any other American who has worked down among the masses of the world in eighty countries more than I have. I am like a soldier reeling from the battle front where we are being overwhelmed.

I feel like weeping over America and saying, "If only you knew what would bring you peace! It's hidden from your eyes." Yet it will not be hidden from your eyes when this meeting is over. Then you must go out and help Chicago see. Open her blind eyes —that is your business when you go out of here. For the fate of America and the world hangs on you and all others like you whose eyes are opened.

The Pentagon cannot do this. They are trained to fight hot wars and drop bombs. They are not trained to win a war like this. China was not captured with a hydrogen bomb or soldiers; it was captured with promises. These masses of people that I know so well in China and all Asia and Africa and Latin America . . . nine-tenths of them are hungry people.

You in America are always worried about eating too many calories. Most of you are losing the "battle of the bulge." But over there on the other side of the world, they are worried about getting one meal a day. They are hungry, sick, unhappy, wretched. And we do not help them. We had our chance to help their hunger, but do you know how many missionaries we sent to help their agriculture? Thirty! Out of five thousand missionaries to China, only thirty were agricultural missionaries. To meet the needs of four hundred and fifty million people, those thirty were not enough. We did do more to help them with their health. We had around five hundred doctors and nurses in China. We lost China because we did not care enough. If only we had known, we could have saved China. Every missionary now agrees with me that if we had only cared like the Communists cared, we could have had China.

Why did I tell you this? Because the same thing that happened in China is now happening across South Asia with an appalling, terrible flying speed, and down to the southern end of Africa right now. I know what I am talking about, because I have just been there. I have worked in all those countries of South Asia and Africa. I worked among these masses; taught thousands of them to read. These people who make trips around the world and come back, meet a few people at the top, but they do not meet the people. I know the people who are going Communist. Now, I have told you this, because you have got to know it first and then you have got to know the answer and act this year.

I shall speak especially on India. That is now the most crucial spot on earth. In 1956 India has her next election. She will have over twice as many voters as we have. She had an election at the same time we had ours. She had more women voting in India than we had men and women voters put together. Over 80 per cent of those people who voted could not read or write. One-third of them voted Communist in the southern half of India because they were hungry. In that area down there they did not have enough rain for five years. I have been in parts of southern India where half the people moved out because they were trying to find something to eat. Many starved by the road. We sent a little food, but not one-tenth enough. That is why they voted Communist. In their next election, the most decisive question on earth is, "Will the majority of the people in India vote Communist in 1956?"

If they do, this is what will happen. All Asia will go Communist and all Africa and we shall have five-sixths of the world against us. Then I despair of our democracy surviving. Perhaps some of you people remember that I prophesied in Chicago the Korean War. People said, "How did you know that?" I was there in Korea. I saw these people mad, frantic, begging our American people not to leave. Any fool would have seen what was coming. If you allow India to go Communist, then Asia and Africa will turn our enemies as China turned enemy. How do I know this? I have been living there. Oh, America, America, if only you knew how to save India!

Well, you can do it, but you have got to do it in a big, big way—bigger than any we have undertaken yet. The Church has got to do this. But the Church must change her pace.

The only organization that was ready after China fell was the United States government. A good many people say the government ought to stay out of such things. I think so too, but the government has got to get in if the rest of us are not ready. Frantic, I went to the church leaders of America. Frantic, I went to President Harry Truman. I said to him, "We Americans have got to promise the world, especially India, that we will help her out of her misery by sharing our technical knowledge or she will go Communist." Harry Truman said to me, "You are talking religion. If I made a promise like that, the United States would not back me. You go out and start a revival." I could not start a revival in America. But in his next inaugural address Truman included that promise. It is called Point Four. Our government is spending a hundred million dollars now all over the world and some of that in India to save India. I believe that helped save India from going Communist. But I do not think the government ought to do this. I think you Christians ought to do it. I think you American people are losing your world because you do not know your own power.

Jesus never scolded people for being bad; he just pitied them for being blind. Notice that. Read all that he said all the way through . . . poor, blind, deaf people with blind leaders. America needs a leader, not in Washington, but in the Christian Church—a leader today to lead you out to a crusade to save the world. You can save it easily when you really try.

I will tell you why I know something about India. The Indian people have three felt needs. One of them is *food:* they are hungry and they want something to eat. I am glad that we are giving as much as we are of our wheat and of our clothing. But I am ashamed of burning potatoes and oranges; I am ashamed to allow scores of ship loads of wheat to rot when the world needs it. We ought to give all of that. I do not see how anybody can feel comfortable with God looking down on us when we do a thing like that. Do you feel comfortable? But we must do far more than give them food. We must show them how to raise their own food.

The second thing that we must do for India is to help improve her *health.* Our government sent a hundred health and agricultural experts over to India from the Mid-West of the United States.

But our government found that the thing the masses wanted most of all was to *learn to read.* They thought the reason why they were hungry and sick and in despair was because they were ignorant. They believe you have secrets in books and they want those books. They want those secrets so they want to read. So the American Point Four invited us of World Literacy to come and help them. I have been with the Point Four program for one year trying to help them with this literacy program, because that is what the masses of India wanted. And I will tell you what we did. Where the beautiful Taj Mahal stands the leading American and Indian technicians met. We said to them, "What are you trying to tell these villagers? You tell us and we will write it in simple language." So, we made a tailor-made set of lessons to help agriculture and health. They said, "Tell them they do not eat the right food, they don't know how to eat. That is the reason they are sick." So we told them they must eat more vegetables and fruit and eggs and milk. The doctors said, "Tell them the reason they all have intestinal trouble." One billion five hundred million people of the world, the illiterate and nearly illiterate three-fourths of the world all have dysentery. It is chronic, they have had it all their lives, they don't know what to do about it. They don't know that flies, filth and bad water cause it. So you tell them that they must not let flies get on their food and they must not have contaminated water. We put all that in our primer.

Then the agricultural experts told us what to put in our primer. The hungry people are grateful for your wheat, but most of all they want to know how to get more out of their land. They don't want to be paupers, they don't want to need your charity, they want to be helped to help themselves, they want your know-how. So, the agricultural experts said, "Tell them one reason they don't have good crops is because they use poor seed. Tell them we will give them hybrid corn instead of the little stuff they have now." So, we put that in our book in very easy little short sentences, only ten new words a day. Our primer is full of these practical things. The experts said, "'Tell them that they are starving their land to death. They never put anything back, not even their cow manure. They dry it and they use it for cooking. They never have any other fuel but cow manure in India to cook with. So they starve their land and as a result their crops have been getting worse and worse for a thousand years. They said, "And tell them also that they must use an iron plow, because their wooden plow does not go deep enough. It goes only an inch under the ground. Tell them if they will use an iron point, they can go down three inches where there is better soil." So, we told them that.

But when they used an iron plow, their bullocks could not pull the plow, because their bullocks were too weak. They never feed their bullocks anything, they just let them eat by the roadside. So, we told them how to feed them to make them stronger. But they were a little too small, so we told them how to breed them by crossing with the best stock from America. So this primer told them ninety secrets. We told them how to take care of their children. It is a very unusual kind of primer, but it tells them the things they need in order to rise out of poverty and disease.

I told you this, because if we could do that kind of thing on a very large scale, we could save India and all the rest of Asia. What I said of India this evening is true of eighty countries. We have got to save them, we have got to lift them, we have got to help them help themselves, to prove that we are their friends. If we do not lift them, we lose them. Therefore, you American people must get back of the programs that are winning friends, like World Literacy and World Neighbors.

I travel over the world for the World Literacy Committee. We are attempting to help the people to help themselves first by teaching them to read. We have found that when we teach illiterates to read that they love us, because they believe that literacy is the way out of hell, the way out of hunger. They want to get out of ignorance and they want to read the books that will help them progress. So, when we teach them to read, we win their friendship.

Every country I visited is eager now to help those people to read, because they are trying to prove to the masses that they are their friends. They are scared to death that the Communists will start a revolution. Millions are learning to read. That gives us another problem: what will they read? We've got to train writers. In Asia they do not know how to write simply like American journalists do. In America we have the most fascinating writers on earth. We are sending American journalists out to teach those nationals in every country to write. And then when we get books and magazines written, we must have many presses, not only big ones, but small ones in all these countries. The kind of offset presses that will print books and papers very rapidly and very cheaply.

Then we have got to get them out to the villages. We are putting in the villages a little twenty-five dollar library now. The books are put in a Standard Oil can. We put in disinfectant so the cockroaches and the silver fish and the termites will not eat those books. We include a bright Coleman lamp. The whole outfit costs twenty-five dollars. Anybody who wants to do something fine can join the Council of Church Women of the United States who are already sending thousands and thousands of those libraries. We need a million and a half of these libraries. We are also placing book vans, these costing three thousand dollars in many countries. This is the kind of thing that will save India. I'm so optimistic because I've seen how easy it is. We have the inside track. Communists can only promise to help the masses over there in India *after* a revolution. But we can do it *now*.

Nehru wants us. By the way, don't believe what you hear against Nehru. Nehru is our friend and he desperately needs us. If he goes down, the Communists go in, and if they go in in India, they will go all over Asia and all over Africa. I was pleased when the *Atlantic Monthly* published those wonderful articles about India. I hope the United States government will cultivate India's friendship and realize that she desperately needs us. She is our sister republic.

I am an optimist also because we have all the technical skill we need in the United States, as well as the money. This is a "war of amazing kindness." If we wage this war in South Asia and in Africa, we can capture those people with love in action. These people are the easiest marks in the world. That is the trouble; anybody can have them with a lie, anybody can have them with a little help. Help them and you can have them— don't help them and they will become your enemies and America will be encompassed about on every side. Your enemies will surround you and they will not leave one stone upon another, because you did not know the day.

Now, I will give you a definite date. By November, 1954, America must be wide awake and moving abroad with an all-out program to save the world. If we do so, India will be saved—within one year!

We have a strategy before me which is too long to read. It is on paper. But it must get into action. If you people would back up the programs that are now trying to help India and the rest of the world, you can save the world. Nobody else but common American people can. That is the reason why you are so terribly important.

I'm an optimist, because the masses want you, those governments want you, we can do it now, we don't have to wait. I am an optimist because God wants us to do it this way. You never felt happy when you built up this terrific military and sacrificed the lives of our boys. You never felt happy because you could not look at God and say, "God help us to blow up Russia." But in this war of kindness, you can look at God and say, "God, help us to love the world into loving us and into loving Christ and to help Russia to see Christ in America." How will they ever see Jesus if they don't see Jesus in us? They will never see Jesus in a hydrogen bomb.

Christ weeps over America. Oh, if America only knew that loving-kindness would bring peace on earth, then we could finally save China back and Russia too. They would turn on their own rulers, if their rulers didn't follow this way. It will be cheap and wonderful to capture the heart of the world with love. That is the reason why you and the other people like you in America are the most important people on earth. The fate of your children and mankind hinges on whether you see and act quickly enough.

Now, you can see that I have not been able to finish this, I have not even started. It has been terribly sketchy, but you will find the book *Wake Up or Blow Up* which tells you the whole story. Give it to your friends.

Here are three things for you to do. *Pray* as you have never prayed before. I guess Harry Truman is right; this needs a revival. Pray for that. Second, *give* as you never gave before. If everybody here would give the price of a meal a week, you would be much healthier. Heart disease is the chief killer in America today and it is because we overeat. If you would give a dollar a week, that would be fifty-two dollars a year for this foreign program, and that multiplied by seven million Christians would be three and a half trillion dollars. And then, go out and *witness*. Wake up Chicago and America. Do your part. I'll do mine. Together we will save the world.

# 10

## New Men for God's New Day

### By WILLIAM C. MARTIN

A FEW MONTHS AGO I HEARD A MAN ADDRESSING A COMMENCE-
ment assembly, using as his subject: "It's the Same Old World."
All of us recognize very promptly that in a real sense it is the
same old world—the same laws of nature governing the physical
world; the same laws of God, which is another way of saying the
laws of nature, governing in the realm of the moral and the
spiritual. And we say tonight, "Thank God, it is the same old
world."

But most people, when they use that term, mean by it: "It's
the same old world and there isn't anything you can do to change
it." The same old world of greed and hate. The same old world
of lust and avarice. The same world that we were foolish enough
a generation ago to believe might someday find its way into a
time of peace and security. But then came a First World War and
then a Second World War, and now a girding of nations for
another world holocaust. The same old imperialisms, the same
old power politics, a few changes in actors but the same old plot.
It's the same old world.

*William C. Martin is bishop of the Dallas-Fort Worth area of
the Methodist Church and a former president of the National
Council of Churches.*

Wherever one opens the New Testament, he finds a group of people living enthusiastically and joyously in the belief that God had let loose a power in the world that's destined to make it a *new* world. One of them said, for example, "If any man is in Christ, he is a new creation. Old things are passed away. Behold, all things are new." Another of these early Christians, a prisoner on the lonely Isle of Patmos, had a vision, and in recording the vision he said, "I saw a new heaven and a new earth."

We cannot account for the amazing, self-sacrificing heroism of those early Christians on the basis of any other fact than that they were quite assured that they lived in a world the like of which had never been before. And I believe it is a part of the Church in every generation to find those elements of life that are different. I speak to you tonight about a new world.

It's a new world, in terms of the fact that we have a new acquaintance with it. Never have we known our world so well as we do now. Thirty years ago a person who had traveled very far from this country, either east or west, was an unusual character, but now there is scarcely a rural community in America that hasn't had from one to a dozen young men who have been to the far places of the world. They've written home about it, they've sent pictures about it, they've come back and reported what they've seen. We have an acquaintance with our world today that we've never had before.

And one of the interesting things about that acquaintance is that we are finding that in other parts of the world they are able to do things which we Americans have never been able to do. We find that commerce with the nations of the world is not simply one of giving, but it's one of receiving. I was in Korea at Christmas time, bearing a word of greeting and of Christmas cheer to our men in service over there, and I was amused at being told that a little while ago a group of American agriculturalists went over to Korea.

They were benevolent minded and they thought that now in view of our relationship with Korea we ought to do all we could to help them. So these experts in agriculture went over to Korea to teach the Koreans how to grow rice. Well, they found after a little exploration that the Koreans were growing about 20 per cent more rice per acre than these Americans had ever been able to grow.

We are becoming acquainted with our world. Not only do we know them but they know us. Thousands of their young people have come year by year to our colleges and universities. They've been in our homes. They've touched our American life, and have gone back to tell about it. The newspapers, the radio, television, is not limited to our continent. Acquaintance is the first step in building world neighborhood.

In the second place, there is today a widening realization of the fact of the essential oneness of our world. Notice, I did not say "Unity." Unity is what we do not have. Unity is what we are striving for. But there's a oneness that we simply can't get away from. I know there are words in our vocabulary like "isolationist" and "isolationism." But they've lost their meaning. They're like so many empty shells that have been washed up on the seashore. The life has gone out of them. Whether we like it or not, there is an essential oneness about our world. At the close of the First World War we attempted to make a plan for the world that left a billion people out of account. You can't make a plan for the city of Chicago and expect it to succeed if it leaves half the people out of account. Never again will we make that mistake. "God hath made of one all nations to dwell together upon the face of the earth."

It's a new world. We haven't gone out to seek it. It's been thrust upon us. What a day this is for the missionary program of the Church! I remember the day when a man who talked about foreign missions was talking about something that was very foreign. But not now. Nobody who stands in the pulpit of a church has to go out and bring this thing in, as if he were dealing with something that's remote and marginal. The only thing he needs to do is just open the door and it comes rushing in. We *must* deal with it. This is a day when the modern means of transportation and of communication have pushed the world so close together that you feel at times as if you could almost take it in your hand, as God does.

In addition to these facts, there is the widening recognition that man apart from God cannot construct a world order that has the elements of permanence and dependability. There was a day when many people thought we could. Some of you are old enough to remember those spacious days in the latter nineteen hundred twenties when we were looking so comfortably forward to the day when man, by virtue of his ingenious mastery in the realm of science, would be able to drive out all the enemies of mankind. In a little while there'd be no more poverty, there'd be no more ignorance, and all the evils that infest our world would be conquered. People were saying, "Just give us time to work these things out, and man will be able abundantly to take care of himself." There were those who said, "If there are people who are benighted enough to give any attention to this outmoded thing that is called religion, we won't quarrel with them. We'll simply smile and wish they were more up-to-date. After all, why worry about the unseen world, why not just take hold of this world we have and bring it up to the Utopian dream."

I need not say to you that no thoughtful person is holding on to such a foolish notion as that in this generation. We are constantly being made aware of the fact of that Old Testament truth, that "except the Lord build the house, they labor in vain that build it."

It's a new world. Some people have not awakened to it yet, but the children of God are coming to understand that even as in New Testament days, there is an awakening that calls forth from us the best there is in us, matching God's new world with new men.

There was a day in my own ministry when I would have been willing to rest the case with a diagnosis of this sort. But I think you recognize that the only justification for such an effort at analysis is simply to give the background for something that needs desperately to be said. In the hundreds of addresses given before the Chicago Sunday Evening Club there has been enough moral and religious truth released, not only to save this city, but to save our entire nation and the whole world. Now what's the trouble? What's the barrier, the blockage, that stands between the revelation of this truth and the capture of the human heart and the transformation of the world order?

Somehow or other there's a lack of communication. We had in this country one summer a young Scotsman by the name of David Read. He wrote a little book called *Communicating the Gospel* and the chief emphasis of that book is that what the Church needs today above all things else is not a different Gospel, not a new revelation, but the opening up of channels by which this Gospel which we have may be carried out into the areas of life where decisions are made, where men and women confront all the problems and the temptations of life. Somehow or other we have failed to keep the lines of communication open.

I wonder if during the remaining minutes you'll allow me to talk in very plain and direct terms concerning the possibilities of an awakened layman. I'm not talking about an official layman. I'm not talking about a man who holds some high position in the circles of his church, either local or denominational. I'm talking about the plain, ordinary, everyday layman who sits in the pew on Sunday morning, and who takes his share in the life of his church as an unofficial layman. Where can he take hold of a world situation such as I have described, in this new world?

Let me say, first of all, he can take hold in terms of his job. If tomorrow morning you should go on the streets of Chicago and find fifty churchmen and ask them the question, "How do you serve God?" you'd meet with a variety of answers. Some would say "I serve God by going to church." "I serve God by contributing to the church." "I serve God by being a good neighbor." "I serve God by reading my Bible occasionally, and I have a kind of sporadic prayer life." I suspect it would be rather unusual if out of those fifty men you found five of them who answered promptly and emphatically, "I serve God with my daily vocation." And in our failure to recognize that simple fact we've lost something, something that came to us through this New Testament Revelation, and was recovered for us in the Protestant Reformation—the sacredness of the day's toil—a man's job, whether he works with mind or hand or both, whether he works in that realm of life that we call the cultural realm where direction is given in a special way to the thinking of his fellow man, or whether he works in some remote area of life where the light of fame never shines and where his name never gets into the newspaper.

In the Christian conception of life this call is not limited to the ministry. We believe, as Protestants, in a called ministry. But we also believe in a called laity. The man who goes about his daily task, that follower of Christ who takes his daily occupation and through it attempts to maintain an economic order in which the possibilities of hopefulness, based upon fair play and justice, are open to every young man for a chance to take the gifts that God has given him and to use them in some creative fashion— the man who approaches his task in that fashion is entitled to know that he stands by the side of the Lord Christ.

We talk about the wild rush of communism across the world.

Communism never comes in except where the soil has been prepared by unemployment, hopelessness, fear, despair, and a sense of futility on the part of the individual.

I said to the men to whom I spoke in Korea, how much we thanked them for the good job they were doing to hold that line. But I also reminded them that the line which they were holding in Korea is not simply a line a hundred and fifty miles long across that peninsula—it's a line twenty-five thousand miles long —it goes all around this planet. And every one of us stands on that line, whether we recognize it or not. We are helping to hold together an economic and a social order at a time when the welfare of this nation is supremely important to the welfare of the world, not simply against communism but against all the "isms" that would come in and disrupt our pattern of fellowship and brotherhood, that would break the bonds that bind us together and would set neighbor against neighbor and friend against friend. A man's job is his chance of taking hold upon this new world that God has set before us.

Second, his tithe. By that I mean that portion of his income, whether it be large or small, which he gives for the establishment of the Kingdom of Christ. During those sixteen days in Korea, I crossed and recrossed a number of times the line that separates the army and the church. Well, it's a rather hazy line in places, because of the marvelous job our G.I.'s are doing in the support of orphanages and churches and hospitals and clinics, and the other agencies that are necessary to give the kind of undergirding to people who have suffered more than any of us in America fully realize.

But, the line is there, and I found myself impressed, and at times depressed, by the wide variation between the resources that are available for the army and the resources that are available for the Church. Of course the answer is easy: the army is supported out of public tax funds, and the missionary is supported by the voluntary gifts of church members. I do not begrudge any dollar that's being spent to keep a soldier warm and well fed in a Korean winter. He deserves the best we can give him, and he's getting it. But I did find myself wondering as you would have done, if there isn't something that can be done to give to the missionary a greater degree of material resources for the doing of his job? And there is. It grows out of this question of Christian stewardship. I saw statistics recently that indicate that from all the people in America in 1953 the total giving for those causes that are related definitely to religious enterprises was less than 1 per cent of our total income. If you take half the people out who do not belong to any church, and divide the total giving by the other half, it still amounts to less than 2 per cent. I must be frank in saying I do not believe we'll ever be able to bring the Kingdom of God into this world on the basis of that kind of meager giving.

Into the layman's hand God has put material resources which, when brought together, in the aggregate will provide the resources for doing the things that need to be done. As I looked upon those vast needs, and thought about the needs in our own country of various kinds, I found myself saying, "We can't do everything but we can do something." Under God I see no way by which a Christian can live with his conscience giving less than that portion of his income which is approved by Scripture and by human experience—the tithe.

His job, his tithe, his witness. If you should look for the secret as to how that New Testament Church spread so rapidly in the face of the most bitter persecution that a great pagan empire could wage against it, you'd find it in five words: "He brought him to Jesus." That was said of one man after another who went out and found somebody and brought him to Christ. My fellow Christians, there'll never be any substitute for that kind of direct approach. No amount of institutionalism will ever compensate for the failure of the individual to bear his own personal testimony as to what Christ has done for his life.

I close with a brief report of an experience that came to me recently in the home of a layman in my home city. He told me about a friend of his, a vice-president of one of the banks of the city, who called him a few days before and said, "I want you to come over and tell me what it is you've found that makes your life so different from my life." This friend of mine has no unusual ability to express himself. He is just an ordinary, everyday layman, who loves God and loves his church. He said, "I went. I went with fear and trembling. But I said, 'I must do my best.' " I wish you could have seen the light that was on his face as he told me how he stood the Sunday before at the altar of the church, when this friend of his took the vows of church membership, having been baptized in the name of the Father and the Son and the Holy Spirit.

Here they are: a new world, God's new world, calling for men at their best. Every man is challenged to offer his job, his material possessions, his witness. With these he can join that host of conquerors concerning whom it was said, "They overcame by their faith."

# 11

# In Quest of a Vital Religion

## By ROBERT J. McCRACKEN

HUMBOLDT SAID THAT IT WOULD COMFORT HIM ON HIS DEATHBED
to have a piece of Homer read to him, were it only from the lists
of the Greek ships. He meant that there is something in the music
of words which adds to their value. It is what one feels about
this magnificent sentence. There is music in it. It has rhythm,
melody, majesty. Paul was not deliberately or consciously a stylist.
It was his faith that inspired such lyrical language. "I know
whom I have believed, and am persuaded that he is able to keep
that which I have committed unto him against that day."

Paul had a vital religion. He was not a secondhand but a firsthand Christian. His faith was not founded on hearsay but on an
experience immediate and personal. Reading his letters you never
have the impression that he is mechanically repeating what he
has heard somebody else affirming, or that his religion is tradi-
tional, conventional, a family inheritance. On the contrary, he
leaves you feeling: Here is a man who in the realm of faith has
made a discovery, who is thrilled by the wonder of it and living
in the glory of it. You note from his use of the first personal
pronoun—"I know. . . . I am persuaded. . . . I have com-

*Robert J. McCracken is minister of Riverside Chuch, New York
City.*

113

mitted"—that his religion, wrought into the texture of his life and thought, passed through the fires of his soul, is his own, his very own.

What made Paul's religion vital? His vivid sense of God; his no less vivid sense, begotten in him by Christ of the forgiveness of his sins; a new sense of power, of adequacy for life; a new sense of peace, an inner serenity independent of circumstance; a new infectious gaiety of spirit, a joy also independent of circumstance, not bound up with health or wealth, temperament or disposition; and especially an outgoing love for others, a desire to serve them and to share with them the discovery that had so transformed his life.

If only all religion were like that! So much of it, as you and I well know, is conventional and formal, without vigor or vitality, more a matter of outward observance than of intimate acquaintance, with little in it to quicken the pulse or stir the heart or constrain to action. It should be a tremendous, dynamic power, sweeping into human life and changing it utterly, but for so many who reckon themselves religious it is no such thing. It has not entered into them or become a part of them. Instead of being the most distinctive and characteristic thing about them it is a kind of addendum, an incidental and marginal interest, nominal rather than vital. They have no vivid sense of God or of having their sins forgiven by God. The transforming power of religion has never been released into their lives.

It would be a mistake to suppose that they are in every case content that it should be so. Deep down in their hearts the religion for which multitudes hunger is a vital religion. If God is to be known they want to know Him. If religion has the secret of the mastery of the art of living they want to be introduced to it. If pardon and power and peace are available, really available, they need them and want to know what to do to get them. How does religion become a matter of firsthand experience? How does one personally appropriate it? How is the passage made from formal observance to intimate acquaintance? What has one to do to secure direct contact with spiritual reality, an original, immediate confrontation with God so that one can say without exaggeration the sort of thing Paul said? "I know whom I have believed, and am persuaded that he is able to keep that which I have committed unto him against that day." I raise the question because in one form or another people have put it to me. I reply to it with four suggestions.

First of all, *consult the experts.* Go to those who have had a vital religious experience and observe what they have to say—how they came by it, how they maintained it, what they conceive it to be. It is what you must do if you want any kind of experience. Musical experience, for example. If you want that you have got to get to know the great masters. You have got to sit at their feet, to live with them, to learn from them, to set yourself to understand what, through their glorious medium, they are saying. It is what you must do if you want scientific experience. Any physicist, chemist, engineer will tell you that there is no shortcut to it. There is no substitue for hard work, for a long apprenticeship of inquiry and application, genius in this field as in any other being an infinite capacity for taking pains. You have got to get down to the study of the textbooks. You have to make yourself familiar with the findings and conclusions of the experts.

With religion it is the same. You don't just stumble on a vital religious experience. It is only acquired, and then developed and deepened, by industry, dedication, discipline. It has its textbooks, covering every aspect of religious experience, some of them ancient—*The Confessions of Augustine,* some of them medieval —Thomas à Kempis' *Imitation of Christ,* some of them modern —Thomas Kelly's *Testament of Devotion,* the greatest of them the Bible. If we desire a vital religion we have got to consult the experts. The measure of our desire can be estimated by the extent to which we do consult them. The prophets have a great deal to teach us, and the psalmists, and the saints. Above all, there is Christ. No one has ever known God as intimately or as fully as he. The Gospels give us his teaching. They introduce us to his principles. In their pages we see him at work. We come under the influence of his mind and spirit. The very atmosphere of his presence invades our lives. This is what others have found. This is what we can find. If you want a vital religion consult the experts.

The second suggestion I make is: *Don't attach too much importance to your feelings.* It is what we all incline to do. We covet the glow of religious emotion, and if we lose it, or experience it only at rare intervals, we are apt to think that the vigor and vitality have gone from our faith. What has to be remembered is that feeling is only one-third of our life. Thought and will are its other constituent elements, and God is apprehended by thought and will as well as in feeling. Religious emotion should not be sought as an end in itself. Because the soul has its moods feeling is certain to vary from day to day. There is such a thing as rhythm in the spiritual life, the swing of the pendulum from free glad communion to seeming dereliction. The glow departs; despondency and depression supervene. Jesus himself passed from the Mount of Transfiguration to the Garden of Gethsemane—yes, and to a Golgotha where he could only say, "My God, my God, why hast thou forsaken me?" Just as in nature night succeeds day and winter alternates with summer, so also in the religious life radiance and gloom, elation and despair are not very far from one another.

It is a mistake to identify vital religion exclusively with emotional fervor or to suppose that it must always be accompanied by ardor and passion. Not intensity but depth and stability are the signs of authentic religious experience, and they come through the patient, persistent exercise of the mind and the will. In vital religion it is the whole man, the entire personality that is engaged. Moreover it is a law of the mind that as the years increase feelings become less intense, but in spiritually educated minds they become refined, because thought and will temper and mature them. Emotions stale, convictions ripen. William Law, author of the great Christian classic, *A Serious Call to the Devout Life,* when he rose from bed at five in the morning, was accustomed to pray: "When I awake I am still with Thee." That was the first doctrinal affirmation with which he confronted his half-awake and half-reluctant soul. Notice that he did not say, "When I awake I *feel* that I am still with Thee." The chances are that he did not. One is not very rich in feeling at five o'clock in the morning. William Law said a deeper thing to himself. He said, "When I awake I *am* still with Thee." Think about that. In religion don't attach too much importance to your feelings.

The third suggestion I make is: *Give God a chance.* After all, if you spend about sixteen hours of your working day in thinking about this world, and a perfunctory five minutes, if even that, in trying to remember your Maker and your immortal soul, this world will naturally seem to you about two hundred times more real than the other. This must be so, however real the spiritual world may be. If you never think of it, or only very occasionally think of it, it will be unreal to you. I want to emphasize that. It is impossible to be worldly-minded six days in the week and spiritually-minded for an hour on Sunday. It is impossible that on our feet we should be selfish, superficial, cynical, and then suddenly become different persons on our knees. John Milton found that if he was to write poetry well he had himself to become a true poem. Similarly, if we want to have a vital religion we must make a real place for it in our lives.

I don't know how often people have told me that they don't pray because God is not real to them. The truth of the matter is that God is not real to them because they don't pray. To the person who never prays God cannot make Himself real. To the soul which will never subdue its noisy clamor to silence, to listen for the divine voice which guides and blesses and reassures, there is little hope that a convincing religious experience will ever come. But to the person who prays habitually, not only when he feels like it but whether he feels like it or not, his will going into action when his emotions flag, God is sure to make Himself real, sure to become the biggest fact in life, filling the whole horizon. If there is one thing the experts are unanimous about it is that.

Brother Lawrence spent ten long years teaching himself to pray, ten years of quiet, resolute, unceasing effort. The chief reason why people give up the quest for a vital religion is because of the difficulties attending the quest, difficulties that are just as much practical as they are theoretical. And back of the practical difficulty lies something deeper. Al-Ghazali, the Moslem mystic, has a sentence that cuts like a knife. "If you are never alone with God, it is not because you are too busy; it is because you don't care for Him, don't like Him. And you had better face the facts." Let us be honest with ourselves about this. Do we really want a vital religion? Are we prepared to pay the price for it?

The fourth and and final suggestion I offer is this. If you want a vital religion, and you haven't got it, *try to find out what is holding you up,* what the block or barrier is which is coming between you and God. The one thing about which you should not entertain any doubt is that God is seeking you with a passion and a constancy which put to shame any search you may be making for Him. We often talk about seeking God as if He were an elusive person, always just beyond our grasp. How much nearer to the truth Francis Thompson was when he daringly described God as the Hound of Heaven, tirelessly on our track, never giving us up, His love refusing to let us go. What we ought to seek are the things which come between us and God. It isn't always a simple matter to put a finger on them. They slip so easily into the unconscious. We are all such born rationalizers.

I once heard Dr. Hutton tell about a young man in his congregation who was forever complaining about his intellectual difficulties in the matter of religion. If it was not the inspiration of the Bible it was the miracles, if it was not the miracles it was the divinity of Christ, if it was not the divinity of Christ it was the inconsistent lives of Christians. For a while Dr. Hutton listened patiently and sympathetically and did all he could to help, but the impression began to grow on him that the difficulties had another source. One day when a fresh intellectual problem was described Hutton looked the young man straight in the eye and said, "Tell me, have you by any chance any difficulties with the Ten Commandments?" It was a frontal attack and it proved effective. It turned out that in that particular case the crux of the difficulty was not intellectual at all; it was moral. Don't misunderstand me. I am not saying that *all* religious difficulties have a moral rather than an intellectual source. I am saying that they sometimes have. They are based on character. They strike their roots into some secret sin. It may be an evil habit which we will not surrender. It may be an illicit relationship which we will not break. It may be an attitude so selfish, so cantankerous, so censorious that it is poisoning all the springs of our spiritual life. I am perhaps talking to somebody now who can put his finger on the thing which he has never surrendered, on the place where he is saying "No" to God. Friend, don't talk about looking for God until you have got that right. Don't rationalize. Be realistic. Be logical. Be reasonable. Don't try to justify what you are doing because to face the facts would be distasteful and a mortal blow to your self-esteem. Ask God to show you the true nature of your sin, how it binds you, how it blinds you, how it comes between you and Him and keeps you from the most powerful transforming influence in the world. When it is recognized, confessed, surrendered, the barrier between God and your soul will have gone.

Let no one say that he cannot attain a vital religion. All of us can if we will. We can have a vivid sense of God and of the forgiveness of sins, a new sense of power and peace, a new infectious gaiety of spirit, an outgoing love for others. I point the way to a firsthand, vital religion. Consult the experts. Don't attach too much importance to your feelings. Find out what is holding you up and break with it. Give God a chance.

Late one afternoon Charles Kingsley walked by the seaside. That evening he made an entry in his diary. "My spiritual birthright! Before the sleeping earth and the sleepless sea and stars I have devoted myself to God, a vow never, if He gives me the faith I pray for, to be recalled." That day Kingsley sought and found a vital religion.

# 12

## Sorrow and Joy According to the Christian Faith

### By REINHOLD NIEBUHR

CHRISTIAN FAITH DOES NOT HOLD THAT GOD DWELLS IN ETERNAL equanimity. Every religion excepting Judaism and Christianity which are Biblical religions insists that the end and the beginning of all things is an eternal calm. But from the standpoint of the Christian faith there is a peace of God that, St. Paul says, surpasses understanding precisely because it is a peace that has pain in it.

The fruits of the spirit are declared to be love, joy and peace. But the whole Christian life is described in such a way that one realizes also that it is not a simple peace and happiness. In the Bible there is a great deal about joy and about sorrow but very little about happiness. We read, "If ye will not die with him, neither will you live with him." We are crucified with Christ and nevertheless we live. Life comes through death, joy through sorrow, "Blessed are they that mourn for they shall be comforted." Peace comes out of strife, "Blessed are ye when men shall revile you and speak all manner of evil against you falsely." Fulfillment through hunger, "Blessed are ye that hunger and thirst after righteousness." There is no simple peace; Christianity is the re-

*Reinhold Niebuhr is dean of the faculty of Union Theological Seminary, New York City.*

ligion of the cross. A cross is revelation of the heart of God and a cross is at the heart of human existence.

Is not this morbid? Could we not have something simpler? The fact is that all of us look for something simpler and the Christian faith has at many times been rejected until the moment of sorrow when there is no other way of finding joy except through sorrow. It is in sorrow that the truth of the Christian faith becomes known. But every one of us instinctively would like to have happiness, simple happiness, rather than this complex thing of joy through sorrow.

Happiness might be defined as the concomitant of the natural feeling tone of any neat harmony of life. Now, thank God, there *are* some neat harmonies. None of us could live without moments of happiness.

By a neat and nice harmony I mean, for instance, the proper harmony of the body when it is healthy and gives one the pleasure of health. None of us can live without some friction with our fellow men, even in the most ideal family life; yet basically, a happy family life is one without essential friction. Many of us thank God for that kind of happiness. There are wider harmonies, too. We have some fairly harmonious communities although one admits when he looks at the wider community of the world that there is not anything very neat there.

There are then neat harmonies such as the harmony of the body and the harmony of the family which give us a certain amount of happiness. Perhaps the man who expounded most profoundly what happiness means was the great philosopher Aristotle. He wrote a whole book on the subject and he proclaimed that a combination of harmony with happiness to be the goal of life. Why should not we attain that goal? Did not our Declaration of Independence assure us of it? Perhaps not quite. It assured us of the right to the *pursuit*. "We hold these truths to be self-evident, that all men are created equal, that they are endowed by their Creator with certain unalienable Rights, that among these are Life, Liberty and the *pursuit* of Happiness." This is perfectly correct and, of course, the philosophy of the eighteenth century which is the background of this wonderful document, held to something more than that we merely had the right to the pursuit of happiness. It also held that we really had a right to happiness itself.

The reason that happiness is not a right, or, at least, that there is no guarantee of its achievement is that there are not very many and not very long neat harmonies in life. The richest experiences of life come out of relationships that have *tension* in them— where things are a little bit askew and where that which is askew is transfigured into something nobler.

Take man himself. He is not a creature meant simply for happiness. He is not meant to be happy because he lives in two worlds. What a contradiction—to be the judge of all things and yet to be a worm of the earth.

Whenever the philosophers try to make man into a simply happy creature, they either reduce him to the level of nature or lift him to the level of mind. Man is a creature who lives on both the level of nature and the level of mind. He brings his "years to an end like a tale that is told" and dies but knows that he dies. He "looks before and after and pines for what is not." Man is a creature who has a memory such as the animal who lives just in time does not have. You know that wonderful poem by Swinburne about the swallow singing so gaily in the summer and he wonders why man cannot sing as gaily and then he comes to the conclusion that it is because the swallow lives merely in the moment and man has a memory.

> O swallow, sister, O fleeting swallow,
> .   .   .   .   .   .   .
> Could I forget or thou remember,
> Couldst thou remember and I forget.

Man is a creature who does remember. He lives in memory and in foresight. His years pass and come to an end and yet he touches the fringe of the eternal. There is no simple happiness for a creature like that. There is glory, there are remarkable tensions but no simple happiness.

The Bible goes on to say that there is a much more fundamental contradiction in man which creates sorrow in him; it is not that he has a body which is in time and a soul which is out of time but it is that man is a creature who contradicts himself because on the one hand he loves himself and on the other he cannot be truly himself if he does not love others. There is tension between my self-love and my knowledge that I ought not to think as highly of myself as I do, that I ought not to center my life round myself and that I ought to give myself to my fellows. Because I do not give myself absolutely to others, I have pain in my life. That is, I have an uneasy conscience; and an uneasy conscience is a form of pain.

Psychiatrists deal with what might be defined as a morbid conscience about fancied violations of real or fancied laws. It is strange that our generation should think that a guilt complex is identical with the uneasy conscience expressed in the words of the Psalmist, "We are consumed by thine anger, and by thy wrath are we troubled."

Recently there appeared a cartoon which showed a big, bruising criminal in the penitentiary with a little chirpy prison doctor saying, "I know what is the matter with you. You've got a guilt complex." This cartoon is revealing concerning the culture of our age.

The Bible says the way to get rid of guilt is not to cover it up but to allow it to flower under God until finally a new life emerges. This is, in other words, the old gospel of repentance. If men allow the uneasy conscience to flower under God's judgment, there can be such a thing as the old self dying and a new self being born and set free. It is part of the process of redemption that instead of being anxious and desperate about ourselves, there is a point in the relationship between man and God where the uneasy conscience so overwhelms the old self that the old self is destroyed and there emerges a new self which has a certain freedom, a certain nonchalance about life. The nonchalance and joy which come out of the pain of repentance belong to the good life. It is part of the Gospel that a new life comes out of the death of the old life.

But now suppose that we say that there ought to be happiness in this new life. Is it not the teaching of the Gospel that we are unhappy if we are sinful and hateful with one another and that we can be happy if we love one another? Can we not have some simple joy or happiness at least in this new life? Well, let us look at this new life again for a moment from the standpoint of the Gospel. We can never profoundly consider the possibilities of peace with happiness and joy without considering also sorrow and pain.

If there is any real integrity in Christian life, there can be no perfect adjustment with all other life. This is another one of those issues on which our culture gets pretty well baffled. Are you perfectly adjusted to all other people? Are you perfectly adjusted to your neighborhood? I hope that none of us is perfectly adjusted to our neighborhood. We do not have to regard ourselves better than the other people who live in the neighborhood, but if there is any real integrity in the Christian life there must be some point or other in these relationships which we have with others, in the shop or in the factory or in the counting house, where we must say to people who may be as conscientious as we are and whom we do not judge otherwise, "Here I stand, I can do no other, so help me God."

Perhaps one of the reasons there is such a tremendous deterioration in public morals is because morals have become too public without enough of a sense of an ultimate judgment beyond all the judgments of man. Remember the great chancellor at the time of Henry VIII, Thomas More? Henry VIII tried to coerce the Church and make it an instrument of politics. He said to More, "Now all the bishops have agreed to this and everybody in the Church has agreed to it and why do you hold out?" And More replied, "If they have all agreed in England, they have certainly not agreed in the whole of Christendom. And if they should have agreed in the whole of Christendom, certainly the Church triumphant as against the Church militant, could not have agreed to this. I appeal to Christians living and dead." This is an example of conscience expressing itself in the pain of disagreement.

I know very well that most of us are not potential heroes or martyrs although there have been good percentages of martyrs since the totalitarian regimes have appeared. But it is pretty clear that in a really totalitarian and demonic community the best you can expect is 5 per cent of the people to be heroic martyrs. This doesn't change the fact that there can be no Christian integrity which does not have some pain of disagreement and some heroism to the point of martyrdom. I may be wrong in a decision in which I disagree with my friends. But there are certain times when I must say, "It is a small thing to be judged of men; he who judges me is the Lord." This is the experience which in sorrow produces an ultimate serenity, a serenity that comes out of a sense of integrity, but it is not a simple happiness. Obviously it is a complex form of joy rather than happiness.

But there is a much greater problem than that. Any real life of Christian integrity must be imbued by love. When a life has been changed from self-centeredness to one that lets go of the self and relates itself in love, there ought to be more, rather than less, love in it. We must not claim, of course, that Christians love their fellow men just because, thank God, the Lord of the universe redeems us by what the old theologians called "common grace," "common grace" being manifest in a kind of family or community relationship which draws me out of myself and saves me despite myself; out of the operation of community life this common grace enters into the heart and saves me from excessive egocentricity. If there is any genuine spirituality in the life that I walk, the further I walk, of course, the more my life relates itself to the pains and sorrows of others. This is the real paradox of love. There is no simple happiness in love, only the joy which comes out of sorrow. Consider the particular anxieties, worries and concerns that are carried by a father and mother, a grandmother and grandfather, nephews and nieces and aunts and uncles and wife and husband of every family. These are the pains we carry because we love other people. The more people we love, the more pains we bear.

When I was a student I was taught that the Stoics in their idealism were closer to Christianity than any other philosophers. This is true to a certain degree. It is also partly false. The one thing that distinguishes Stoicism from Christianity is the central point of my present theme. The Stoics believed in equanimity—complete equanimity—and the way to get it is to cut yourself off more and more from other life so that there will be no distraction.

One of the greatest Stoics was Epictetus, a Roman slave who became a philosopher. This is what he said about the perils of family life, which shows the distinction between Stoicism and Christian idealism:

A wise man should be without distraction. He should not be tied to vulgar duties. He should be entirely attentive to the service of God. Consider, if he is married, there are some duties due to his father-in-law, some to the other relatives of his wife, some to the wife herself. He is obligated to the care of the members of the family whenever any of them are sick and to making provision for their support. Let us speak of other things. He must have a vessel and warm the water to bathe his child and there must be wool, oil and a bed for his wife after her delivery and thus the furniture of life increases. More business. More distraction. Must he not provide clothes for his children? Must he not send them with pens and ink and paper to the school master? Do you see how this brings our wise man down and how it robs him of his kingdom?

Now you will have to admit that this is a very accurate description of family cares by a man who presumably had no experience of them. And it is also a very explicit disavowal of them. The difference between Stoic idealism and the Christian conception of joy through sorrow appears in the solemn joy which an anxious mother has as she keeps vigil over a sick child. You remember that Abraham Lincoln wrote one of his most beautiful letters to a mother who had lost five sons in the Civil War. He wrote to her about "the solemn joy that must be yours to have laid so costly a sacrifice upon the altar of freedom." In this case Lincoln, as so frequently, caught the spirit of the Bible, the solemn *joy* that must be yours, not happiness.

We have talked too much about the right to happiness in our civilization. Some of our soldiers in Korea may think they are not there for a good cause. But whether they are there for a good cause or not, many of these boys have been promised happiness, even individual happiness. But they can have no simple individual happiness because they are part of a vast civilization and they cannot have it now because if they have it at all it will be something which comes of what things may be. Happiness is not for them. And for that matter, not for you or me either. It is a silly notion that our life depends upon neat harmonies and the feeling tone that comes out of them. Life is full of terrible and tragic contradictions including the contradiction between you and myself when we do not get along with each other, which can only be healed by the harmony of forgiveness which has pain in it. In the end that is the most wonderful kind of joy.

Perhaps I can gather together all that I have been saying in the words that Jesus spoke when the disciples of John the Baptist came to him and said, "What a difference there is between you and John the Baptist. We do not know which one to accept. John the Baptist is a very severe and terrible man and you seem to be a man of joy." "Do not let that disturb you too much," answered Jesus. "The difference between us is not as great as you imagine. You remind me of a little song that children sing when at play in the street, 'We have piped upon you and you would not dance. We have mourned unto you and you would not lament.' John the Baptist came neither eating nor drinking and you said he had the devil in him and I came eating and drinking and you called me a gluttonous man and a wine bibber." The point in the comment of Jesus is in the words, "We have piped unto you and you would not dance; we have mourned and you would not lament." "Be careful," Jesus was saying. "You are the kind of people who can neither dance nor cry because dancing and song come out of the same sensitivity that tears come from." If there is really a sensitive heart which has been touched by God's grace, it will weep many a tear and will rejoice in many a song. The love, joy and peace of God all contain the pain and sorrow of the cross.

# 13

## The Lord's Prisoner

### By G. BROMLEY OXNAM

A YEAR AGO, WHEN I HAD THE HONOR OF ADDRESSING THIS splendid audience, I had just returned from India where I had been attending the Central Committee of the World Council of Churches. It met in Lucknow. And strangely enough, I have but recently returned from the Executive Committee of the World Council of Churches, this time the meeting in Germany at Koenigsstein, just outside the city of Frankfort, Germany. There we took final decisions concerning the plans for the great Assembly that will meet here in Evanston upon the Northwestern University campus.

I am not to talk about the World Council of Churches this evening, but I think I state the fact when I say that the second Assembly will prove to be the most significant event in the religious history of this nation. We'll begin on Sunday evening, when a hundred thousand people, we believe, will be in Soldier Field. There in a service of worship the great themes of redemption and of salvation will be dramatized as the Assembly itself opens. The six hundred delegates from one hundred sixty-one churches from nearly fifty nations will be here, and six hundred

*G. Bromley Oxnam is bishop of the Washington, D. C., area of the Methodist Church.*

130

accredited visitors, a hundred fifty consultants, a hundred youth delegates, and thousands of others will be coming here. The theme will be "Christ—The Hope of the World." It will be an event of the utmost significance. As an American, I'm happy in the thought that these religious leaders from all over the world are to see your country and mine as it is. There is an aspect of the World Council meeting not often expressed, namely, that as these hundreds of leaders of the great churches of the world move back into their own communities and record what they really see, more good will be done in terms of international understanding than many at present understand.

Going to the Executive Committee this time—you'll pardon me for being personal—Mrs. Oxnam and I decided we would fly over a few days before the sessions, so that we might spend a brief time in Rome once again, and in Florence. Many here have visited Rome. We visited the Mamartine Prison, where, according to tradition, the Apostle Paul stood in chains. We went to the Coliseum and in imagination it was peopled with the tens of thousands who were there in the days of the Caesars. We went to the nearby cell where the Christians prayed and sang hymns and then moved into the arena to die as martyrs. We went, as many of you have gone, to the spot where it is believed the Apostle Paul was executed. And it came upon me as it never has before, this: the place of the prison in the history of Christianity.

Take the New Testament itself. How many letters of the New Testament were written by men who at the time were in prison. Paul concludes the letter to the Colossians with these words: "Remember, I am in prison." Then he says, "Grace be with you." What can you do with a man like that? "Remember, I am in prison. Grace be with you." If you take the New Testament that is related to men who suffered imprisonment, or were in prison at the time they wrote, you take most of the New Testament—if you call the roll of the centuries, it is hard to name a century in which Christians were not in chains.

At the Executive Committee of the World Council of Churches, once again I saw Niemoeller, eight years in the prisons of Hitler; Berggrav, who stood before the Nazis and refused to bow; Lilje, one of the most courageous of the prisoners of Hitler! And as I speak to you this evening, many of you will recall that our dear and distinguished friend, one of the bishops of our own church, is in prison in China tonight, Bishop Chen.

I want to talk to you about the Lord's prisoner. Prisons have had a place in our Christian history, and it may be that we will be called upon again to suffer for the faith. It is challenged today as perhaps at no time in history. It is going to take courage. It is going to take conviction. It is going to take a willingness to stand, as you will find in one of the letters of the apostle to whom I am to refer this evening.

The Lord's prisoner! I'm talking about Paul. He's on the road to Rome, and you remember there was disaster on that voyage. The ship was wrecked and it seemed for a time that he would never reach Rome even as a prisoner. These words are quite interesting in the Moffatt translation: "It was only after our escape that we found out the island was called Malta." There was a shipwreck. "The natives showed us uncommon kindness, for they lit a fire and welcomed us all to it, as the rain had come on and it was chilly. Now Paul had gathered a bundle of sticks and laid them on the fire." That's interesting to me. The apostle who laid the foundations for the Christian Church in the Roman Empire was not above building a fire. He laid the sticks on the fire—"when a viper crawled out with the heat and fastened on his hand. When the natives saw the creature hanging from his hand, they said to each other, 'This man must be a murderer! He has escaped the sea, but Justice will not let him live.' However, he shook off the creature into the fire and was not a whit the worse. The natives waited for him to swell up or drop down dead in a moment, but after waiting a long while and observing that no harm had befallen him, they changed their minds and held he was a god." Isn't that strange! One moment a man is a murderer and the next moment he is a god! There is a shifting public opinion that we need to hold in mind.

The governor of the province welcomed him to his home. The governor's father was ill with dysentery and Paul healed him, and then there's this very interesting note: As they were about to leave, "they made us rich presents and furnished us, when we set sail, with all we needed." I can't read the whole story, because I want to deal with this Lord's prisoner in another way if I may. "In this way we reached Rome. As the local brothers had heard about us, they came out to meet us as far as Appii Forum and Tres Tabernae, and when Paul saw them he thanked God and took courage. When we did reach Rome, Paul got permission to live by himself, with a soldier to guard him." What did that mean? It meant really that he was chained to a soldier in a private house that he had to pay for. And then this last—and this is the reason that I have read this to you, "For two full years he remained in his private lodging, welcoming anyone who came to visit him; he preached the Reign of God and taught about the Lord Jesus Christ quite openly and unmolested."

I've often wondered what Paul talked about in those days. Here he was in the city of Rome for two full years before his execution, and people came, and he talked about the reign of God quite openly. What did he really say? No recording device in those days. How amazing it would be, how marvelous, if we could have recorded what Paul actually said in those conversations. What wouldn't you give to hear Paul repeat the 13th chapter of I Corinthians! But all we can do is to turn to the letters he wrote, this prisoner of the Lord, to find out what was in his mind.

I read you two or three verses and you will find that we'll move from the first century to this century very, very quickly, because some of the words of the prisoner of the Lord have to do with you and with me in this particular hour. In the letter to the Ephesians he says this: "As the Lord's prisoner"—he wasn't ashamed of it—"as the Lord's prisoner, then, I beg of you to live a life worthy of your calling, with perfect modesty and gentleness, showing forbearance to one another patiently, zealous in love." Then he speaks of our hope. He says we have "one Lord, one faith, one baptism, one God and Father of us all." This is what he talked about, I think, when people came to see him. He said this—doesn't it strike you as a bit strange?—"Copy God, then, as his beloved children, and lead lives of love, just as Christ loved you and gave himself up for you to be a fragrant offering and sacrifice to God." He actually says to you and he says to me, "Copy God."

And then when he writes to the people living in the city of Philippi—it was there that the first church of all Christianity in Europe was founded, there the first convert to Christianity was won—we find him writing in a little different fashion. The Lord's prisoner says, "I know how to live humbly; I also know how to live in prosperity. I have been initiated into the secret for all sorts and conditions of life. . . . In Him who strengthens me, I am able for anything." This isn't some individual who is not involved in the strife of the day. This is from a prisoner, the Lord's prisoner. "In Him who strengthens me, I am able for anything." No wonder this man went through to the very end.

Here is a verse all of you know very, very well, but I read it to you this evening, coming from the Lord's prisoner, out of a prison centuries ago, because he is speaking to free people in these United States in these days, "Finally, brethren, whatsoever things are true, whatsoever things are honest, whatsoever things are just, whatsoever things are pure, whatsoever things are lovely, whatsoever things are of good report; if there be any virtue, and if there be any praise, think on these things." How simple!

*"Whatsoever things are true."* We're living in a day in which men have learned to tell the big lie. The Fascist found out how to do that, the Nazi learned how to do it, the Communist knows how to do it—to tell a lie, and repeat it and repeat it, until at last the sheer reiteration of the falsehood breaks down resistance, and after a time people begin to repeat the lie as though it is the truth. You remember when George Orwell wrote his book called *1984* he pictured the tragic moment when the totalitarian takes over a great free country, and he said the first thing that was done was this: they took from the dictionary every word that would express the concept of freedom, until at last there was no vocabulary by which an individual could longer voice the idea of freedom. The big lie. Will you forgive me? It seems to me for the first time in our history we ourselves are beginning to forget whatsoever things are true. There are those among us who are beginning to tell the big lie. And we now have the instrument by which the big lie can be propagated. It is possible now for one man to speak to tens of millions of people, and if it be he does not remember whatsoever things are true, he has means to propagate the falsehood and the people are in darkness.

Take, for instance, the careful broadcasting of a man like Edward R. Murrow, Erwin Canham of *The Christian Science Monitor,* or Elmer Davis of the American Broadcasting Company, and compare it with the partial, the propagandistic, the partisan broadcasting that you find coming from certain individuals today who have the privilege of the air, and have learned the technique of the big lie. Whatsoever things are true!

May I give you an illustration for a moment of what I mean? I have here a card. You can't see it. I wish you could. In some ways I'm glad you can't. On this card is a picture. It is a picture of a white man. You see him here with his head, his forehead developed, he's handsome. Superimposed upon this picture is a black man. He's shown with slanting forehead and little brain, thick lips. And on the back of this, being distributed by an agency that talks about Americanism and talks about Christianity, I find these words—the big lie—listen: " 'All men are created equal' is a Communist statement." I thought that was written into the Declaration of Independence. I thought the idea that all men are created by the Eternal and in His image, beings of infinite worth, is a Christian doctrine. I thought that Americans were conceived in liberty and dedicated to the proposition that all men are created equal. But this is being circulated in the name of Americanism. I read you the rest of it. It's astounding. " 'All men are created equal' is a Communist statement. No two objects in nature are alike. The more alike, the lower the form. Likeness is a sign of abasement. Negroes and Asiatics are very similar. All lower races are. They consequently have very little culture. Variation indicates where God is working and choosing. The white race built civilization because it has variety and is able to reflect the infinite creative spirit of God. Negroes and Asiatics are catalytic. You cannot raise them, but they will lower you. They have destroyed many white civilizations by breeding into them. Communists spend millions of dollars in the United States to make you think Negroes and Asiatics are the equal of whites. This sort of propaganda will destroy the civilized world. The lower human forms are unable to reflect the infinite capacities of the civilized mind. If form meant nothing the dog would be as smart as a man. Variety of form and variety of races is God's way, not equality of races. What the lower races have, the white man gave them. Do you protect your white child from the Communist lie that all races are equal?"

May I suggest to you, that's the beginning, in its anti-Semitism, in its anti-attitude toward the Negro, that's the beginning of a big lie. Whatsoever things are true. We need to remember what the Lord's prisoner said.

When we were in Koenigsstein in Germany, there at the Executive Committee of the World Council, the foreign ministers were also in Berlin. We were deeply interested of course, as Americans, and even more deeply interested because John Foster Dulles had been so closely related to the World Council and to the National Council of Churches. We listened, and I think it is fair to state that at no international conference of recent years has our leadership been excelled. When Mr. Molotov made his statements, so many of them spurious, they were not allowed to pass. Every day there was a succinct and devastating answer coming from Mr. Dulles, and what was he doing? He took the propaganda stage away from Mr. Molotov. We took the initiative. And Mr. Dulles, our Secretary of State, was speaking to the millions of people in China and in India, and doing an extraordinarily effective job. And what happened? When he came back home, those who have mastered this technique of the big lie, because he had done what we had hoped might be done, had worked out a conference at Geneva where we might sit and possibly end the Korean conflict and the Indo-China war, those who don't understand we live in a world and we've got to work together, began to undermine with the lie, until this distinguished Secretary of State was held up before our people in some quarters as having failed at the moment perhaps of his greatest success. Whatsoever things are true.

The American people wish the truth. In an hour of this kind, an hour of crisis, our leaders must learn, and our press must learn, and our radio must learn, all who reach the public must learn, whatsoever things are true, think on these things.

I give you one other illustration and then have to move on quickly. We have heard it said that twenty-two hundred and forty-seven people have been dismissed from governmental service, alleged to be security risks. Some say twenty-four hundred. I don't know whether it's twenty-four hundred or twenty-two hundred and forty-seven. I have no knowledge. But I heard the former governor of Illinois over the radio make this statement that after studying some two millions of our governmental employees, they have found one alleged active Communist. I don't know whether that's the fact. But I'm using the illustration to say this, that the time has come for us to recognize that it can't be twenty-two hundred and forty-seven, and one. Somewhere something's wrong there. Whatsoever things are true.

The American people are an adult people, capable of receiving the truth, and we want it. We'll make up our minds and we'll make our own decisions in the light of the truth. The big lie has no place in American life, and a prisoner of the Lord of centuries ago is speaking to us with power today.

*Whatsoever things are honest.* There is no question whatsoever about the complete right and duty of the Congress to conduct investigations. No one debates that. Congress must investigate in order to have the information upon which to base sound legislation. That's a proper and necessary function. While one doesn't question the propriety of Congressional investigation, there is a fundamental demand for honesty. The real purpose ought to be so to understand the menace that does lie in the Communist threat, that we can legislate intelligently to get at the causes, to deal with the effects, and to move out. But there is good reason to believe that there are all too many who are capitalizing upon hysteria for political advantage in an hour when the nation is in peril. Whatsoever things are honest.

I give you an illustration here that ought to stagger the American people. These procedures are not honest. They are incompetent and irresponsible. I can give you one illustration. A prisoner of the Lord speaks out from yesterday. Whatsoever things are true, whatsoever things are honest. In the last report of the House Committee on Un-American Activities I find one of the great women leaders of Christianity in this nation listed as an identified Communist. One of the distinguished leaders of the Young Women's Christian Association, a woman not a Communist, never having been associated with the Communist movement, anti-Communist in spirit. Why is her name there? Because in a secret hearing a witness who has become a professional witness, at least he has testified again and again, this individual said that this lady, according to his knowledge, had been a member of the Communist party. She was never heard. She didn't know that the testimony had been given. She was never notified. He of course was not cross-examined, but upon the basis of one man's statement in a secret hearing, unverified and unevaluated, a distinguished leader of religion is listed today as a member of the Communist party. I suggest to you that isn't honest.

We need today to deal with the psychological factors that underlie the Communist movement. We need to turn to those who can meet a philosophy of materialism. When I listened to your distinguished chairman putting before us the threat that we do face today in the new weapons that are ours, we've got to meet not only an expanding imperialism, but an infiltrating ideology, and it's necessary to remember that while you need strength to hold back an expanding imperialism, you've got to have ideas to meet an infiltrating ideology. Why can't we be honest enough to turn to the philosophers like Reinhold Niebuhr and Sidney Hook, and Bishop Sheen, who know the threat of materialism, to find an answer to the materialism of the movement? Why can't we turn to the great leaders of labor like Walter Reuther and George Meany to learn from them the methods that were used in driving this threat from large areas of the labor movement? Turn to the resources that are available, be honest. In a word, to deal with a situation that is too menacing to trifle with. Whatsoever things are honest, think on these things.

*Whatsoever things are just.* When will we realize that the truest way to make our society impregnable in an hour of attack is, under the conditions of freedom, to establish justice and thus be on the road toward a fraternity? I give you another illustration. You saw the announcement in the paper that a distinguished Negro leader of the city of Chicago has been appointed Assistant Secretary of Labor. I happen to have the privilege of knowing Mr. Wilkins. I performed the wedding ceremony in which one of his sons was married to a daughter of the minister of the largest Methodist Church in New York City, St. Mark's Church, a great Negro church. And when I performed that wedding ceremony the mother told me that of her three sons the first had graduated from college, the University of Chicago, when he was sixteen. The second had graduated from college, the University of Wisconsin, when he was seventeen. The third had graduated from college at eighteen. The mother said to me, "My sons ran down hill intellectually as they came along." The sixteen year old went to Harvard and received his doctor's degree in physics, with honor. Then he studied with Einstein at Princeton.

Recently in the city of Baltimore at a great conference on human rights, led by the representatives of the labor groups of that city, I said: "Surely we can start with this, that a man's right to earn his living ought to be determined by his character and his capacity, never determined by his color or his creed." That's just a simple beginning, the right to earn one's living. And yet I find some people in the name of justice aren't willing to stand for this simple principle. Does this boy, brilliant in physics, stand before closed doors, or do we open them?

Think on these things. I conclude with these words: "Put on the whole armour of God, that ye may be able to stand against the wiles of the devil. For we wrestle not against flesh and blood, but against principalities, against powers, against the rulers of the darkness of this world, against spiritual wickedness in high places. Wherefore take unto you the whole armour of God, that ye may be able . . . to stand." The prisoner of the Lord!

# 14

# The Door to Life

## By HAROLD COOKE PHILLIPS

IT MUST SEEM TO US THAT OUR LORD HAD SUCH A STRANGE WAY of winning followers. Whenever we want to win anybody to our cause, our party, our club, our church, we put the best foot forward. We appeal to their self-interest. We point out the advantages that would accrue to them should they accept our invitation.

How different was Jesus' method! What bait did he hold out? None at all. This is what he said to the people whom he wanted to follow him: "If any man will come after me, let him deny himself, and take up his cross, and follow me." While England was passing through her darkest hour Sir Winston Churchill sought to rally her by challenging his compatriots with "blood, tears, and sweat." So our Lord never appealed to the softness in people, always to the heroic. "If any man will come after me, let him deny himself."

In the first place let us say something about this self of ours. You see, the trouble with the self is that it is always with us. We can't get away from ourselves. If we have a disagreeable neighbor we can move away from him. We can never move away from

*Harold Cooke Phillips is the pastor of the First Baptist Church, Cleveland.*

ourselves. If we go to the uttermost parts of the earth, we take ourselves along. St. Augustine found this out in his spiritual struggles. He said, "I remained to myself as a luckless place, where I could neither stay nor get away. Whither could I flee from myself? Whither should I not follow myself?"

I think there is no doubt that many of us turn to drink because it's such a speedy way of escaping ourselves. The trouble with that is that the escape is only temporary. Moreover, after each excess, the self with which we still have to live seems less desirable to be lived with.

What then does one do with oneself? What attitude adopt? Many answers have been given. The hedonist, the man bent on pleasure, says, "Enjoy yourself." The teacher says, "Educate yourself." The artist says, "Express yourself." The philosopher says, "Know yourself." Christ says, "Deny yourself." And not only does the Christian religion say this. East and West, Buddhist, Hindu, Confucianist, Christian—all tell the same story. We might truly say that a large part of the spiritual wisdom of the race is that *self-denial is the road to selfhood*. Certainly this is one of the major insights of Christianity: that self-realization comes through self-denial.

Let us then think about self-denial. It seems on the face of it such a strange road. It seems such a negative, repressive attitude. Indeed, how can one reconcile this idea of denial with the abundant life which Christ offers us? If the aim of Christianity is abundant life, how can one get life by saying "No" to it? How can one experience life when one denies it? Self-denial, it seems, would imprison us rather than liberate us. It would bind us rather than set us free. It plucks our wings, and cramps our style, and blocks the full free flow of the current of life. It dams up the waters that seek the fullness of the sea. So it seems.

There are two facts, however, that we should consider before we come to this conclusion. For one thing, we must remember that each of us has at least two selves. Plato described man as being a charioteer that drove two horses, one white and tractable, the other black and fractious. Robert Louis Stevenson has immortalized for us the man of dual personality, Dr. Jekyll and Mr. Hyde. When H. G. Wells says of one of his characters that he wasn't so much a human being as a civil war, I think we all know what he was talking about. Because in most people there is a constant tension, there is a fight between these at least two selves of which we are composed.

I read recently of a boy who applied for a job as an usher in a theater, and the manager asked him, "What would you do in case of a fire?" "Oh, don't worry about me," said the boy, "I'd get out all right." Well, that self is in all of us. But not so long since I read about a boy in Korea, who was given the Congressional Medal posthumously. Once when he was ambushed he exposed himself and drew the fire of the enemy so that his buddies could escape, and that self too is in all of us. One self asks, "What is there in it for me? Nobody, nothing matters, just so my own self-centered, self-seeking wishes are satisfied." And the other self says, "Greater love hath no man than this, that a man lay down his life for his friend."

Now since each of us possesses two selves that are so different, it is obvious that they can't both be of equal significance or worth. One of them, like the genuine coin, rings true, and the other is counterfeit. Christianity teaches that the real self is the heroic self. Jesus, incorrigible optimist that he was about human nature, told the story once about a boy who went into a far country, mired in the excesses of his lust, and he said, "When he came to himself"—his real self, his noble self—"he said, 'I will arise and go to my father.'" Christianity maintains that in goodness and truth and beauty one encounters reality. It regards evil as an intrusion, as being spurious and rotten and ultimately self-defeating. When therefore one speaks of self-denial, he has to ask

himself, "What self are we thinking about? What self am I denying? The self that is counterfeit or the good self, which is the real
self?"

Before we regard self-denial as being a repressive sort of thing
there's another fact we ought to consider, namely, not only do
we have two selves, a mean self and a generous self, a cruel self
and a kind self, a clean self and a dirty self, but also this: that
when we refuse to deny one kind of self, automatically we are
denying the other. Perhaps I might make this clear by an illustration. Many years ago it was my privilege to take a trip down
the River Rhine. It was a beautiful sunshiny day. As the little
boat wended its way around the curves of the river one could
enjoy the beautiful foliage, or the little villages on the banks of
the river at which the boat stopped occasionally. Moreover, with
his guidebook one could learn a lot. He could identify the old
historic castles that stand on the hills overlooking that river. One
landmark of special interest was the rock, famous in song and
story, from which the Lorelei is said to have lured the boatmen
to their doom. During the entire trip down that river, four American tourists sat below deck in a smoke-filled room, playing
bridge. They would not deny themselves the pleasures of bridge.
Ah, but think of what they were therefore denying themselves. If
one will not give up the pleasures below deck, he will automatically give up those above deck. Because this is a law of life:
*whenever we say "Yes" to something, automatically we say "No"
to something else.* And when we have the moral courage to say
"No" to something, we then say "Yes" to something else.

A man, for example, may choose to live the life of a philand-
erer. He will throw all restraint to the winds. He will stop at
nothing in indulging his passions and enjoying the pleasures of
the senses. The word "discipline" simply isn't in his vocabulary.
He will not deny that self. Ah, but think of what he *is* denying
himself. He's denying himself the chances of a happy home, the

love and respect of a good woman. He's depriving himself of the deeper experiences of beauty, loyalty and friendship. When he says "Yes" to one kind of life he automatically says "No" to another kind of life.

A potential athlete might, for argument's sake, be very fond of club carousals and midnight suppers. He may also have a desire to make varsity. Very well, he can't have both. If he does not deny himself his gastronomic and gregarious proclivities, he *will* deny himself his letter.

Now when you put these two things together—the existence in all of us of two selves, a low and a high, a good and an evil, and the further fact that when we refuse to deny one of those selves, automatically we are denying the other—then we come to see that self-denial, far from being a repressive idea, is a positive force, far from barring the gate or shutting the door on life, it opens the door to life. It is through this kind of self-denial that men have explored the deeper areas of life and reached its higher peaks, discovered the life abundant.

Observe further that what we have said is true not only of the individual life, it is true also of our collective life, our social life, our corporate life. I wonder if we might not have a hearing on an issue that is very much in our minds these days—the methods of our investigating committees. No one questions the right or indeed the bounden duty of our government to ferret out and expose the foes that may be in our own household. But surely we have got to find some method of doing this without continually smearing the character of loyal American citizens. This task is too difficult and too delicate for men whose yen for publicity and hunger for personal power obscure both their vision and their judgment. If we do not deny ourselves that sort of thing, we shall deny ourselves what our Founding Fathers referred to as "the blessings of liberty" which they "bequeathed to posterity." And it is a fact that we are losing some of those blessings. I know beyond any shadow of doubt that there are many Americans today who are afraid to say publicly what they think, because we have almost come to regard dissent as treason, and disagreement as disloyalty. Religion teaches that the end never justifies the means—it teaches that the means determine the end, and if in our attempt to defend freedom, we continue to employ our current methods, we shall find that we are not defending freedom, we are destroying freedom.

And I think the same thing holds true not only of our country. It holds true of our world. I think if Christ could speak to our world today, which is hovering on the brink of possible destruction, he might say to us something like this: "You would not deny yourselves your hundred per cent nationalism, your boasted sovereignties, your racial bigotries, your economic creed and exploitation, your worship of power. Therefore you have denied yourselves a co-operative society in which men can live in reasonable security and peace."

Consider finally, that if Christianity lays down self-denial as being the door to life, both individually and collectively, it is because through this door Jesus himself passed to life. I sometimes think that as you and I consider the life of our Lord, the perfection of it and the beauty of it, we must think that he just fell out of the sky already made. We're wrong if we think that. He was in all points "tempted like as we are, yet without sin." He "learned obedience through the things that he suffered." He grew, "increased in wisdom and stature, and in favor with God and man." Surely self-denial was the door through which he passed to that matchless character and timeless life.

Think of some of the things that Jesus must have denied himself. He denied himself the safety and security that might have been his, had he been willing to remain indifferent or mute before the deeply entrenched evils of his day. He denied himself that. Ah, but see the prize he won. As a result, he has become the supreme symbol of truth and of justice. He has done more to awaken the social concern and the conscience of man than anyone who ever lived. Any man today who boldly stands for right against wrong, who defends the weak members of society, the underprivileged, against exploitation, any man who does that finds in Christ his unfailing strength.

Jesus denied himself the acclaim of the crowds, the quick and cheap popularity that might have been his and was within his grasp. Had he been willing to give the people what they wanted, to share their petty prejudices, and to flatter their nationalistic pride, and to encourage their vain hopes, he could have been a national hero. He denied himself that. Ah, but see the prize he won. As a result, he has become the one truly universal character in history, the Man to whom all men look when they seek brotherhood, "the true Light that lighteth every man coming into the world."

Jesus denied himself the luxury of revenge, the satisfaction of getting even, and of returning evil with evil. Ah, but as a result he has become for us a symbol, the greatest symbol of God's forgiving love.

He denied himself the indulgence which tempts every normal man, the riot and excesses of the senses, and the allurement of sin, but as a result, we call him our Saviour.

Self-denial a negative, repressive fact, closing the door to life, barring the gate of life? Ah, no. It's a positive force. It opens the door on life. This is what Jesus teaches us—teaches us not only with his words—teaches us supremely through his Cross and his Resurrection. Because it is in the light of the Resurrection that we come to see God's intention for us, and the truth that "beyond every crucifixion there is a new and a better life." A new and a better self rises from the dead. "I die daily," said

Paul. It is as we have the courage to nail to some cross the evils that seek the destruction of the real self, that the God-self, the good self, rises from the dead.

Some time ago the walls of an old cathedral in Europe were being cleaned and under many layers of dirt and grime was found a very lovely picture. I believe that picture is in every man. God painted it. It is the image of God on our souls, but only God knows how we can overlay that, hide it, through our indulgence and our sin. "Give the best in you a chance," says the Master. "Say 'No' to evil. Deny that self." And whenever we say "No" to evil, we are saying "Yes" to God, and so to our real self.

# 15

## How to Handle a Sense of Guilt

### By JAMES A. PIKE

SOME OF THE THINGS IN THE GOSPELS MOST DIFFICULT TO BE-
lieve awhile back are now becoming the most modern and
sophisticated teachings. For example, we read, in St. Mark's
Gospel especially, how Jesus drove out devils. Today we talk
about something called schizophrenia—split personality.

Now, what does that mean? It means that your usual normal
personality is grasped by an alien, distorted and destructive
center of consciousness. What is that? Well, some call it a devil.
I'm not sure the word "schizophrenia" is any clearer as to what
it is. Then there is that condition which is known as multiple
schizophrenia. It's not very common, but it means that you have
personalities A, B, C and D all mixed up in you. You remember
the case when our Lord challenged the inner life of a man and
asked him to name himself and the answer was, "Our name is
Legion." Multiple schizophrenia!

So, too, Jesus tells the sick man, "Thy sins are forgiven thee.
Rise up and walk." Today, we have a better knowledge of the
unconscious levels of man's existence, through the science we call
depth psychology, and its applied form—psychoanalysis. Through

*James A. Pike is dean of the Cathedral of St. John the Divine,*
*New York City.*

the knowledge of psychosomatic medicine we see the relationships of the unconscious layers of our spirit to our bodily health. So, it is not at all mystifying to learn that a man who has been helped to handle his sense of guilt in the right way, is able to get up and walk when he could not before.

I am going to talk about this one relationship, because it lies at the center of the human problem. I am talking about your problem and mine when I ask a question which can be phrased this way, "How can I have self-acceptance and self-criticism at the same time?" Now you may think that's an abstract question, but think about it for just a moment and see if it isn't your main problem. How can you see yourself honestly as you really are and at the same time accept yourself? Because if we do not have self-acceptance, we cannot live with ourselves; and if we do not have self-criticism, others can't live with us.

The problem lies in the area of guilt. If we judge ourselves honestly, if we examine our consciences, if we try to see what sort of people we really are, then we make ourselves quite uncomfortable. We can't face it. This is because it is absolutely necessary that I accept myself if I am to carry on, if I am to be confident and joyous, if I am going to be effective. I've got to be able to accept myself, or otherwise I am running on two cylinders. Yet if I allow myself to know me and if you allow yourselves to know each of you—each one's own self—then how can any one of us accept ourselves—because no one of us is acceptable.

There was a very patient psychoanalyst who spent many, many hours with a woman (with the patience that only members of that profession are capable of mustering), and after a time even he lost his patience and he said to her, "Madam, you don't have any inferiority complex, you *are* inferior." When the time comes that we recognize *that* in ourselves, then where do we go from there? We don't want to recognize our own inferiority and so we cover up in a variety of ways. I am going to suggest some of the "cover-ups" we use.

First of all, I try to lower the level of morality down to suit my own measure. If I can get the *ought* down to the *is* level, then I don't feel that tension which we call guilt; so I say something like this, "Well, I am as good as the next fellow, you know." Or I establish some set of rules like "I pay my taxes and I don't kick my neighbor's dog." Or "I'm a good Elk" or "I'm a good Rotarian." We settle for a set of good manageable rules and then we feel less uncomfortable about ourselves. Or we find some specific way of justifying our conduct. "Well, you see, I was a dead-end kid; I never had a chance," or in more sophisticated terms, "When I was nine years old I had a traumatic experience and, so, I am the way I am, you see."

That is one way. The most common way that the reviewers dealt with the famous Kinsey Report was this: A lot of people do a lot of things we thought were wrong; so I guess they're not wrong any more. There is a modern translation of one of the verses in I Corinthians 13—that famous passage on love—which says, "Love does not rejoice in the statistics of evil." You see, we often do rejoice in the statistics of evil, because by them we can find that we are not so bad; or else that there is no bad and good, which is even more comforting.

Now, why do we do this? It's all right to criticize the rationalizations, but this doesn't go as far as we ought to go, because we still rationalize. Perhaps in bed at night, we go over some of the things that have gone on during the day and we feel sort of shabby about the way we've acted toward people or the way we've done our job. My particular vision at night is usually my desk—which is generally a mess, a lot of letters and notes and little pieces of scratch paper. I say, "I have not done those things I should have done." I didn't make a phone call that someone was relying on. I talked five minutes with somebody I should have spent an hour with and I talked an hour with someone I should have spent five minutes with. Now one of my little pet phrases to comfort myself is, "Well, there are only twenty-four hours in the day, you know. A man can only do so much." And, this makes me feel more comfortable, I suppose. But why do we do this? We do it—and I go back to my first point—because it is absolutely necessary that we accept ourselves. We must, or we can't go on.

But the trouble with this particular way of accepting ourselves is, first of all, that it keeps us in the ruts we're in. We keep on doing the same things and having the same bad tempers. We tell ourselves, "You see, I've always had a bad temper, that's the way I am," so we don't change. We keep on being objectionable to people and we never quite find out why a lot of people don't like us, because we never allow ourselves to face ourselves. There's one side of our problem. The other side is more complicated and something we can understand better these days through these new sciences I referred to earlier.

When we make these excuses, it does not get rid of the sense of guilt, it simply puts blankets on it and lets it sink right down into the unconscious and there it remains and festers. It makes us sick in body as well as in spirit. Now, if you want to test that sometime, go on a long vacation. Particularly if you have been very busy for a long time. You see, if you are very busy, you keep the lid on the unconscious. You keep things from popping up into the conscious levels. You keep all this hidden. But let your mind relax, with no golf clubs or tennis rackets. The first week or two you are too tired to permit much of anything to happen— but then notice what happens. With the activity ceased, the layer between the conscious and the unconscious relaxes and you will find your mind entertained with a veritable floor show of demons.

Events of twenty years ago that you thought you had covered up become clear images.

What can you do about it? What is a healthy way to handle a sense of guilt?

Four years ago my wife and I built a little summer place on Cape Cod. We arrived in our station wagon with our four children late at night, and knowing there would be a lot of problems the next morning, we had the foresight to stop at a little general store along the way on the outer Cape. In addition to getting enough things to see us through breakfast, I had the foresight to pick up one of these little triangular holders you put in the corner of a sink. After a day or so, that was full; so I made a special trip into town and I got one of these containers that you step on and the top goes up. We put that in the corner of the kitchen and three days later that was full. My wife said to me, "You know, Jim, we are going to have to get at this thing more basically." I said, "All right." And I drove into town again. I got a great, big galvanized can—two of them, in fact. I brought them back in the wagon and we put those in another corner of the kitchen. No problem, at least for a week. Well, now what do we do? You know, it's very funny, but actually that's exactly the problem of the guilt. You can't leave it around the conscious levels, just as you can't leave food around the kitchen spoiling. We don't dare lock it up in the closets, because it will make us sick. You don't dare suppress your sense of guilt, but yet you can't have it around. You can't keep it with you. You've got to get rid of it.

By the way, you may be interested to know how we solved our problem on the Cape. We decided that we would have to have an outside agency take it off our hands. Now, this is the answer to your problem and mine. The heart of our faith is the belief that our God has the resources of taking in to Himself all the hurt, the sin, the guilt of the world. Now there's a great claim, but that's the heart of our faith; that God can take up the hurt of the world. More specifically for Christians, we see in the Cross of Jesus Christ the proclaiming of this great and mighty act of God for us and our salvation; but we don't claim that God was only like that at that moment in history. Uniquely He is then acting for us, but God has always been like that. Time will not permit me to illustrate it in the Old Testament, but if you have time later and wish to see more of how God had always been like this, read the Book of Hosea when you get home. God takes up the slack between His righteousness and my condition. In Christ especially we see God meeting us where we are. In Jesus, God translates Himself into the language of human life and He meets me where I am, "just as I *am,* without one plea." Not as I *ought* to be, but as I *am.* He takes up the slack. He meets me where I *am.*

Now, this is the Gospel. Gospel means "good news." It is not good news that Jesus taught us a very high ethics. The Sermon on the Mount is not good news. There are times when I hardly keep the ethics of Confucius. It is not good news to raise the level higher, though Jesus did raise it higher and thus made clear our need of help from on high . . . *The good news is that high as the ethical demand is, God meets me where I am, because I cannot rise to where He would have me be.* This is the good news. Of course, it looks like a sort of free ride; yet we miss the point of it if we think that's the end of the story.

The Christian religion teaches that good works are not the *means* of salvation, because I'm not that good, but that good works are the *fruit* of salvation. Good works are my grateful response to God's free gift of salvation here and now. What does salvation mean? It comes from a Latin word meaning *salus,* it means health, wholeness—psychosomatic totality, integration, adjustment. It means being "all right." It means being able to accept myself and still be self-critical. God gives this gift and my free grateful response to that is to want to be more like the person I am not. He takes me to be righteous, and now in my gratitude I want to be more righteous. In technical theological language this is called justification, that is, being taken for right when I am not right, just like dealing with a child. I count the child better than he is and he, more often than not, will rise to the picture which I have painted of him. God so deals with us.

Then, the sum total of this in my own personal psychology is, *I can accept myself because God accepts me though unacceptable*, and hence I have the power and the confidence to become more acceptable. It takes a little humility to deal with God on that basis. Not on my own merits, but by His grace. That's the Gospel.

If we understand this, we can understand the words of Sören Kierkegaard, the great Danish theologian of a century ago, who said, "The Christian religion is this, the profound humiliation of man, the boundless love of God, and endless striving born of gratitude." The profound humiliation of man, the boundless love of God, and endless striving born of gratitude.

This gives you some clue as to how you might sleep better at night. One reason we don't sleep so well is that when we go to bed we think over all our unpleasant experiences and then seek to justify ourselves. Then there are the records we play to ourselves, the old familiar excuses, the old familiar lies. I have slept much better since I became a Christian a few years back and understood this Gospel. What I do is this, I examine my conscience every night, I go over the day as best I can. I don't tarry, I don't grovel and wallow in my faults, but I go over them, try to understand them and then, in confidence, I tell the Lord, "Dear God, you are going to be awake all night anyway, you take care of all of this and I am going to sleep. And if I do sleep well, tomorrow I'll be able to serve you better." He does take care of it. He is the outside agency who picks up the garbage of my life. I don't have to carry the trash of my life along with me all my years, going back over it, sorting it out, attempting to get rid of it, attempting to hide it. No, He takes it away. It is better to have it collected daily. A well-run kitchen is organized that way. In our personal lives, we dare do no less.

I selected the final hymn to help preach this sermon; so please don't sing it just as an ordinary hymn. I want you to think about it, ponder it and review in your mind anything I may have said that may help you to accept yourself and still keep a fresh, honest self-criticism. Now, this old hymn was written before we ever heard of depth psychology. Sometimes I am reminded of the man who at the age of fifty looked up the word "prose" in the dictionary and realized that he had been speaking "prose" all his life. As a matter of fact, St. Paul was the best depth psychologist of them all. He said, "There is a different law in my body than there is in my mind and those things I would do, I don't seem to do, and those things that I would not do, are the very things I find myself doing. Who will deliver me from the body of this death?" The psychoanalyst? Perhaps, but he relied upon Jesus Christ, the lamb of God who taketh away the sins of the world.

So, in this hymn, we see that it is God that bids us to come. He knocks on the door before we even know that we need Him. In the second verse we see that there is many a conflict, many a doubt, fightings and fears, within, without—this is the whole problem of the depths which disturb us so mysteriously and make us ill.

And in the next verse we find that He welcomes, accepts, pardons, cleanses, heals, relieves—and then in the last verse we see that He is taking up the slack, is meeting us where we are, He "hath broken every barrier down." Even in our walls of rationalization, the walls of defense we have put around ourselves, our own attempts at justification, He meets us just as we are.

Just as I am, without one plea,
But that Thy blood was shed for
    me,
And that Thou bidd'st me come
    to Thee,
O Lamb of God, I come!

Just as I am, though tossed about
With many a conflict, many a
    doubt,
Fightings and fears within, with-
    out,
O Lamb of God, I come!

Just as I am! Thou wilt receive,
Wilt welcome, pardon, cleanse,
    relieve;
Because Thy promise I believe,
O Lamb of God, I come!

Just as I am! Thy love unknown
Hath broken every barrier down;
Now, to be Thine, yea, Thine
    alone,
O Lamb of God, I come!

# 16

## The Truth That Makes Men Free

### By LISTON POPE

THE LIBERTY BELL IN PHILADELPHIA HAS ENGRAVED ON ITS SIDE a verse from the Book of Leviticus: "Proclaim liberty throughout all the land unto all the inhabitants thereof." Over the portals of the Town Hall in New York City is inscribed a verse from the Gospel according to St. John: "Ye shall know the truth, and the truth shall make you free." These two Biblical inscriptions, on two of our best-known American symbols, belong together. Contrary to the popular belief that freedom means lack of restraint of any kind, true freedom can be achieved and preserved only when it is based on that which is true about our lives and our world. Proclaimed simply in its own name, liberty almost invariably runs to license, and at last to self-defeating anarchy. If America and the world are to have a new birth of freedom, as Lincoln prayed, it must be brought about under a higher loyalty to truth and to God.

Let it be granted at the very outset that devotion to truth has not always seemed to promote the passion for freedom. It is notorious that those intellectual and social systems that professed to have achieved truth most completely have often been enemies of human freedom. For example, the ancient philosopher Plato

*Liston Pope is dean of the divinity school of Yale University.*

sat down to write a description of an ideal republic in which truth would be the final ruler, and he ended with a strict censorship of nearly all mental and spiritual activities within his ideal republic. He went so far as to require a list of properly authorized bedtime stories, and to prohibit certain types of music and of musical instruments. For example, all "soft and drinking harmonies" were to be banished from his good society. (I'm quite certain that "Sweet Adeline" would have been regarded as subversive.) With even greater gravity Plato declared that all atheists and materialists and others who deny the existence and the goodness of God shall be given imprisonment or even death. For Plato, truth alone has the right to be heard, and freedom to be in error is an intolerable doctrine.

Many other guardians of so-called truth have been enemies of human freedom. The medieval inquisition, confident that it knew the truth with theological exactness, defended it by secret hearings, the torture of witnesses, the condemnation and burning of books, and on occasion death by hanging or burning at the stake. Our own Puritan colony of Massachusetts, having defined true orthodoxy, rigorously stamped out all dissenting opinions, driving out free spirits like Roger Williams, thereby helping to populate Rhode Island and, interestingly enough, to create religious freedom in America.

In our own time certain great social systems, professing to have found new truth, have abolished the right to a dissenting opinion. This was true of fascism with its hideous doctrines of race and of power. It is no less true of communism. Having equated truth with its own system, communism tolerates no divergent opinion on any significant question. Nation after nation in Eastern Europe and in Asia has seen freedom fall before the advance of Communist dogma.

"Ye shall know the truth, and the truth shall make you free"? Ah, history is strewn with records of the persecution and the tyranny of those who thought they were possessors of truth. It is of some comfort in retrospect to point out that these tyrants were arrogant and incorrect in their pretensions, and that the truth they presumed to have found was subsequently shown to have been partial or even false. But in their own time and circumstance they considered their views to be absolutely correct. So it almost seems that Jesus should have said, "Ye shall *think* ye know the truth, and that truth shall make you an enemy of *freedom*."

Warned by such dreadful examples from the past, our modern democratic nations have turned Jesus' statement around, making it read, "Ye shall have freedom, and freedom will automatically lead to truth." The emphasis has been placed on freedom, to the virtual neglect of truth. The great emphasis, in short, has been on freedom from restraint. At best, this emphasis has resulted in extraordinary achievements of the human mind and the human spirit: the great flowering of science, creative impulses in the arts, new experiments in religious experience, and the rise of political democracies around the world.

But at its worst modern freedom has resulted in freedom from responsibility. Many of our democratic institutions pride themselves primarily on their freedom rather than on their accuracy. The Town Hall in New York seems to consider that it is more important to defend the right to an opinion, however obviously wrong, than to test opinions in the light of facts. In my own kind of world, a university, furious debates can be aroused over possible infringements of academic freedom, but failures to extend knowledge and to teach responsibility are sometimes tolerated as being part of the price of freedom.

Surely freedom is a prerequisite to the advancement of knowledge. But it has by no means been demonstrated that it will automatically produce truth—or even preserve it. Liberty has been used as often to distort or to ignore truth as to defend it or extend it.

This is true, is it not, in our individual lives? Have we not often used our personal freedom to be untrue to our own best selves? Personal freedom can lead to a higher integration of life than any external force could ever produce, or it can lead to the sort of person like one of Mrs. Humphrey Ward's characters, who was, according to her, more nearly a civil war than a human being. Personal freedom can be used to tear life apart, so that we become no longer true even to ourselves.

In politics, overemphasis on liberty leads to extreme nationalism, under the principle of the self-determination of peoples. Accordingly we have built eighty-five sovereign nations on a planet hardly big enough for more than one. I'm told that the only man-made object on the earth that would be visible from the planet Mars is the Chinese Wall, a symbol of the ancient barriers man has erected against his fellow man. Now assuredly nationalism is true to some of the facts of our broken world, but it is not true to the larger facts of our mutual dependence on each other.

In economics, emphasis on extreme freedom—*laissez faire*—has often proved disastrous to an economy. The truth about an economic system includes the central purpose that it should serve all the people equitably, and utter preoccupation with economic freedom has often obscured and hindered that result.

In religion, freedom has been guarded so jealously, as it should be, that the religious community has been split into innumerable contentious groups, causing men to scoff at any pretense to religious truth in the face of a divided witness. It is well that there should be more than one interpreter of the ultimate mystery, in view of the magnitude of the mystery and of the fallibility of human interpreters. But it seems hardly necessary that American Protestantism alone should have more than three hundred exclusive pipelines to the mind and will of Almighty God.

In nearly every realm of modern democratic life, in short, liberty has tended to run riot, and the restraining bonds of order and of truth have often been ignored or broken. Freedom of speech is twisted into freedom to tell lies publicly, as in much contemporary advertising and political campaigning. Freedom of the press, while taken seriously by a great many publications, is also used to protect special interests, and as an excuse for slanting the news and for suppressing facts. Freedom of assembly becomes a precious sheltering arm for citizens; but it also serves as a refuge for cliques and claques that care nothing about freedom and seek only to exert power. Congressional immunity, which amounts to freedom of a senator or a congressman against reprisal, protects the genuine servant of the people; it also shields misrepresentation and distortion of every sort, and in these latter days it appears to be used primarily for that purpose.

All these freedoms are precious in themselves. They become pernicious only when divorced from responsibility, responsibility to the service of one's fellows in the light of an order of truth that surrounds us all. Ah, Freedom, how many crimes have been committed these latter days in thy name!

In revolt against the excesses to which modern democratic freedoms have often been carried, large sections of the world have swung back all the way to the other extreme, sacrificing freedom for some kind of fixed security or order or compulsory equality. This reaction is a central feature of our times, seen especially in fascism and in communism.

The United States, suddenly realizing that she is the last and greatest outpost of liberty in a dangerous world, has become obsessed recently with the quest for the roots and the extension of freedom, and with the struggle for its extension and its preservation against the Soviet Union. And so it is that we have Freedom Houses, and crusades for freedom, and Radio Free Europe, and sermon contests for the best sermons about freedom, and so on and on. This obsession on the part of Americans has led to a good many very cheap definitions of the way in which freedom is to be preserved. To judge from advertisements in our newspapers and our slick paper magazines, freedom consists principally of being able to buy a new washing machine or a new automobile, or to invest your savings in gilt-edged securities. We are trying to strike blows for freedom in all sorts of superficial and mechanical and external ways. Our current commandments for the preservation of freedom might go somewhat like this:

Thou shalt manufacture hydrogen bombs, and they will keep you free.

Thou shalt suppress the Communist in thy midst, and that will keep you free.

Thou shalt return in thy colleges to an emphasis on American history, that thy youth may be instructed in their heritage of liberty rather than in ceramics or accounting.

Thou shalt keep the alien from thy shores by McCarran Bills, lest an occasional undesirable come to this nation so largely colonized by undesirables.

Thou shalt stir up suspicion and fear in the land, that men may be afraid to voice unpopular convictions, and that freedom may therefore be entirely safe.

Thou shalt require loyalty oaths, to insure that public employees and university professors are either patriots or liars.

Thou shalt have no other gods before free enterprise, and it shall be dangerous to take its name in vain.

Now several of these commandments have real merit, but obedience to any or all of them will not preserve freedom in our land, to say nothing of extending it in the world. Nor shall we stop communism merely by such external and mechanical and political gadgets. We shall not stop communism merely with Marshall Plans or North Atlantic Pacts, or Point Four, or bread or machines or atom bombs. These may all be urgent necessities, and Russia might perhaps be stopped thereby. But communism consists also of loyalty to a set of ideas, false as they are, and communism can be stopped only by loyalty to truer and nobler ideas—truer because they are more nearly in harmony with man's situation in the universe, nobler because they seek to elevate the human spirit rather than to regiment it.

Is it not time for us to discover the deeper wellsprings of human liberty? The drought is long extended, and our reservoirs are running dry. That challenge from Goethe's *Faust* which he called "Wisdom's last fruit" falls on our ears with special insistency: "What you have inherited, that earn, in order to possess. He alone deserves freedom, life as well, who must daily conquer them anew."

Clearly we must learn that true freedom does not depend simply on the absence of external restraints. Freedom is never simply a negative thing. The absence of restraint is only a precondition of freedom. Enduring freedom can result only from positive loyalty to objects that are worthy of the loyalty of free men.

You see, a freedom that consists only of your right to choose as you *please* soon creates its own bondage, because today's choices limit tomorrow's possibilities. Freedom always results in bondage to *something,* or else in sheer anarchy. This means that every act of freedom must be exercised within a framework of loyalty, unless it is at last to be meaningless and self-defeating. Freedom carries no compass of its own; its North Star is Truth.

Suppose, for example, you decide to exercise your freedom by stepping in front of a train. You are quite free to do so—once. But the truth about trains is that they will kill you if you do that. Or suppose you decide to show that you are a free agent by drinking all you please. You can do that too, for a time, but soon you may drink more than you please, for the truth about alcohol is that it is a habit-forming agent. Or suppose you decide to demonstrate your own independence of conventional morality by engaging in sexual promiscuity. You may get away with that too, for a time. But the truth about human beings is that they are not toys, and eventually your own dalliance will turn to stern duty. Or suppose you exercise your undisputed freedom to discriminate against some other person because of race. You may succeed in doing so, but your children will learn the truth that men cannot be treated as less than men. And so in countless areas of life; freedom must always take into account the ultimate truth about human life and its relationships, and about the universe itself, or it becomes no real freedom at all.

You can be free from ignorance only if you are loyal to truth. You can be free from disease only if you obey the laws of health. You can be free to be yourself only when you are loyal to yourself. You can be free to worship God only when you believe in His greatness and His goodness.

David Lilienthal has reminded us recently that our freedom in America rests on more intangible but more enduring foundations than a particular form of economic enterprise or of political procedure. It rests, he said, on moral and spiritual foundations. Could he have meant what Jesus meant when he said, "Ye shall know the *truth*, and the truth shall make you free"?

This truth of which Jesus was speaking was not a neatly formulated code of theological or social principles, by which some men were to beat other men over the head for unorthodoxy, a bludgeon of inquisition and censorship and tyranny. Rather this liberating truth of which Jesus spoke is an ultimate and eternal order of reality, the final truth about the universe itself, always represented, for Christians, in Jesus Christ himself—an order within which freedom never defeats itself, because the chance for its own exercise is never fully exhausted. It is an order of truth that seeks to include all men, not to exclude doubters. Jesus put freedom in a cosmic setting. When you are loyal to eternal truth, Jesus is saying, then and only then you shall be free. You will have the freedom of an eternal city, already building though invisible on earth. You will find your own freedom in loyalty to Him whose service is perfect freedom, and whose will is our peace.

There is no compulsion that you and I should serve this ultimate truth, this order of reality called "God." Even in this basic choice we are left, by God's own design, as Edwin Markham put it, "in tragic loneliness to choose, with all in life to win, or all to lose." But before us as individuals, and before our nation this day, have been set great issues, overwhelming demands for our ultimate loyalty, and on our answering choice depends our bondage or our freedom, according to One who said, "Ye shall know the truth, and the truth shall make you free." What of Him and His authority? Strange paradox, that He who could not avoid a cross was the freest of all the sons of men.

> Thou seemest human and divine,
> The highest, holiest manhood Thou.
> Our wills are ours, we know not how.
> Our wills are ours, to make them Thine.

# 17

# Take Your Share

## By RICHARD C. RAINES

SOME MONTHS AGO HALFWAY BETWEEN HAWAII AND WAKE
Island, in the middle of the night in an airplane filled with
military personnel, I looked out and saw the wing tip. As I could
see nothing below or above, I felt very lonely, insecure and im-
potent. When in this mood, I have found it helpful to turn to
my New Testament. I chanced to read the Second Letter of Paul
to Timothy. I suppose I had read the words twenty or thirty times
before, but this time they seemed to leap from the page, lay
heavy hands upon me, put me in duress, and demanded that, as
the price of my release, I should listen to their message and share
it with others. Tonight I seek once again to be a free man.

The words are an ideal preacher's text in that they contain
the theme and the three suggestions of the message. The words
are these: "Take your share of suffering . . . for the Gospel
. . . in the power of God."

Take your share of suffering. These words do not fall upon
the ears of an American audience with ready acceptance. We, in
America, are an island of unbelievable luxury in the midst of a
vast ocean of indescribable misery. The very statistics prove it if

*Richard C. Raines is bishop of the Indiana area of the Methodist
Church.*

we will listen to them. We have about 6 per cent of the inhabitable space of the earth and 7 per cent of the world's people, but 37 per cent of the world's goods. We have 50 per cent of the world's capital goods, 81 per cent of the world's bath tubs, 79 per cent of the world's radios and 97 per cent of the world's consumption of aspirin and phenobarbital.

The typical American attitude toward suffering is to bear it, when it is thrust upon us, with whatever fortitude and patience we can muster. But here we read in a book, which we have come to revere as the Word of God, that we should "*Take* your share of suffering." It is as if the book would say to us, "There is a vast amount of suffering in the world which if we do not take our share of it, other people will have to carry more than their share."

It has been my sad and saddening but inspiring privilege to be in sections of the world where there is intense suffering and some of it for your and my sake. It would do every civilian good to spend half a day in the Tokyo Army Hospital. You have been in hospitals many times but were you ever in a hospital where there were no women patients, no aged patients, no children patients, no sick people in the ordinary connotation of that phrase—just young men who two weeks before were tough enough to have played on any football team and now are broken, bruised and maimed for life?

It is not easy to look upon a young man who expected to play professional baseball with his right arm gone; or a young man who was playing professional football with his right leg mostly gone. I talked with one young man so guileless, so friendly, that one could not believe that he was in any sense a killer, and yet his right arm was gone just above the elbow. After we became better acquainted he opened up his bathrobe and showed me his chest and stomach. They looked like my mother's old-fashioned apple pie—she used to draw two lines down the center and then make little lines out from the center lines—so it was with him, two red lines down the center and many little lines where shrapnel had been removed.

I moved up to the Korean front and was at the foot of Triangle Hill just a day or two after our boys had taken it. Around me were the evidences of where the shells had been falling all the day before and the day before that. They might begin again any time. About two hundred yards away the shells were falling on top of the hill where I could see our men as they hit the dust. As our great shells would go overhead one could hear a strange WHUSH! ! as if a small jet plane had just passed over—the mortars would go off, like a string of little firecrackers on the Fourth of July, only with such intense concussion that would lift one involuntarily to his tiptoes in apprehension and fear. I saw a small group of our men start to come down the road from the foot of the hill as they were being relieved by other men who were going up. I got out my kodak and thought I would take some pictures of our men with a light in their eye, spring in their step, joy in their countenances, as they were being relieved and coming back to security, to dry clothes, to safety.

I took the pictures, but I saw no such expression on any man's face. There was no joy in the face or light in anyone's eye, or spring in anyone's step—they had been up on Triangle Hill for forty-eight or sixty hours, kept awake all night long by the enemy artillery for there were no adequate bunkers there at the time. They were kept awake all night long by the probability or actuality of hand-to-hand encounter. They were weary, they were cold and wet. They shuffled along, shoulders drooping, arms hanging down, feet lagging, with no expression in their faces, hardly knowing where they were going. They were taking more than their share of suffering.

I saw the Korean people suffer as few nations have been called upon to do so in the world's history. There are about 3,600,000 people in Chicago so I am told. Supposing that all 3,600,000 were ordered to leave tomorrow morning for southern Illinois, for Kentucky, for Missouri, because this city was to be a target of an atomic bomb. All was to be overrun by the Communists. That is what happened in Korea. Nearly 4,000,000 people fled from their homes and in the awful cold of winter. Remember we are in Korea, not in Illinois, and therefore we have no automobiles. There is no system of roads by which we can go, only the main supply route up which the trucks are coming. There is only one railroad and the Army is making use of it. Supplies are coming up and the wounded going back. We must walk carrying everything on our back in an A frame or in an improvised wheel barrow. It is the dead of winter. We must take whatever bedding we are to sleep on and under at night. We must take the food that we will need for at least two weeks. We must take whatever fuel we will need to cook our food and of course some money and some precious family treasures. The new baby must go strapped to mother's back. Grandpa and grandma must go.

So the next morning we start off. Grandpa and grandma have to rest twice during the morning. They must rest three times in the afternoon. It becomes evident to everyone that if the family adjusts itself to the pace of grandpa and grandma they may not make it. The next day looking back they realize that grandpa and grandma said an unusually affectionate good night to them and in the morning when they awakened grandpa and grandma were not there. Some time in the night they got up and left their quilt and blankets and together went out into the cold of the mountains and the snow to die, in order that their family might live. This happened not only once, it happened thousands of times. A million people died on the trek south in Korea.

When I think of Korea I think of a little ten year old girl who was separated from her mother and father. When the trucks came up the main supply route she dashed to one side of the road and they to the other. She never found them again but she attached herself to a woman who was carrying a baby on her back and also leading a little two and one-half year old boy. The mother accepted her as her own, fed the children as mothers will and did not eat enough herself. Then finally exhaustion and the cold overcame her and she sank beside the road and died. So also the baby on her back. But this little ten year old girl picked up the two and one-half year old boy, put him on her back, wrapped a quilt around him and staggered along with him for more than a week, begging food, protecting him until at last she found security for them both.

When I think of Korea I think of a little five or six year old boy I saw in Pusan one cold December morning. I was warmly dressed. I had on shoe packs and two pairs of heavy woolen stockings, woolen underwear, civilian pants and field pants, a woolen shirt, a woolen sweater, a pile jacket, a field coat. I had on a cap with earflaps and lined gloves and I looked out of my car and saw this little five or six year old boy out on the sidewalk in front of his home, dressed in a thin summer jersey that came just above his navel. He had nothing else on. His sturdy little buttocks and legs were purple pink with the cold and his legs were like pistons going up and down as he danced on his tiptoes on the icy sidewalk trying to keep himself warm, trying to keep himself alive.

You will not wonder that he haunts me at night. That I vowed when I saw him that when I got back home to my fellow country-men, I would tell his story, confident that there were thousands of people who would want to send this little boy a pair of pants and a pair of shoes. It costs five dollars to do that. If you want to and can, in addition to what you have already done, you can send a gift to the Sunday Evening Club and I will see that it gets to that little boy or to another equally needy Korean lad.

The people of Korea are simply unbeatable. Twelve or fifteen miles behind the line I saw three farmers in ankle-deep ice water reaping their rice. They had been at it all day long. I looked in on a girl's dormitory at Ewha Woman's University, a room eight or nine feet square, not big enough for one American boy or girl. Seven Korean girls were living there. Seven girls could lie flat on the floor at night and be covered over with a blanket and therefore seven girls lived in that room. No complaints. Happy, joyful, grateful.

The 5 per cent of the people in Korea who are Christians are the force that holds things together and will make possible democratic and freedom-loving unity in Korea in the tomorrows.

What is your share and mine? I do not know that this happened in Korea but it could have. A little boy had grown up in a family so poor that there was only one glass of milk a day for the whole family. Each child was taught how deep he should drink, in the glass, so as to have his share and leave some for the others. Disaster hit his community. He was separated from his family, taken to a Red Cross feeding station, where a nurse gave him the first glass of milk, all his own, that he had ever had. He didn't know that it was his and holding the glass he looked up at the nurse and said, "Mam, how deep shall I drink?" She with a lump in her throat and understanding in her heart said, "Son, drink as deep as you can." What is my share? The answer is, "Drink as deep as you can," because there will be many little boys and girls homeless and cold after we have all taken our share.

Take your share of suffering . . . *For the Gospel.* This is another strange combination of words. Suffering. Gospel. We think of the Gospel as the good news, and it is. We remember how it came at Christmas time, the heavens riven and spilling angelic music, and the angel saying, "Fear not, for I bring you good tidings of great joy." The Gospel is true to life and has in it suffering and joy.

The Gospel is good news about how to live an abundant life in this world just as it is, and also, how to live in the next. Jesus said to us, "If any man would be my disciple, let him deny himself, take up his cross, and follow me." He was seeking to say to us that the Cross is not simply something great he did for us in the yesterdays. It is gloriously and wonderfully that. But the Cross is also something which he began in the yesterdays and which we are to continue. He tells us to carry our cross, not to make our lives melancholy, narrow, inhibited or unhappy. In fact just the opposite. He tells us this because he has discovered that the deepest joys which human hearts can know come only on the other side of the door where we begin to carry a cross. There do we find the ecstasy in life beside which all other joy is tame and tepid.

And then our Lord would also have us prepare for the life which lies beyond. When he described the Last Judgment, you remember, he pictured himself as separating the sheep from the goats and saying to those on his right hand, those acceptable and pleasing unto God, "Come ye blessed of my Father, inherit the kingdom prepared for you from the foundation of the world for. . . ." For what? Did he say, "For you were a Bishop, or a Methodist"? Did he say, "For you were a Catholic," or "For you were a church member," or "For you were rich, poor, educated, uneducated, white, colored"? He went far below to fundamentals and said, "For I was an *hungered* and ye gave me meat; I was *athirst* and ye gave me drink; I was a *stranger* and ye took me in." The righteous amazed, almost interrupt him and say, "Lord, when saw we thee an hungered and fed thee, or thirsty and gave thee drink?" Our Lord must have smiled and said, "Friends, don't miss the point, you didn't actually do it to me but inasmuch as you did it unto the least—the least lovable, the least grateful, the least likely to pay it back—the least of these my brethren for whom I died, ye did it unto me."

That which makes us acceptable to Almighty God and pleasing in His sight, is the extent to which we have been aware of the troubles, the difficulties, the burdens, the hardships, yes, and the ambitions, and the dreams, and the hopes of the people who live right around about us and out to the far ends of the earth. And more than this, the extent to which, being sensitive to these things, we are willing to inconvenience ourselves to lift these burdens, bear these troubles, help realize these dreams, hopes and ambitions.

The Gospel asks us for the sake of our own joy here on earth and for our eternal welfare to learn the possibilities of joy, through suffering, "O joy that seekest me through pain." The Gospel knows of joy in the absence of pain. Little children have this joy. It tells us of joy in spite of pain; courageous adults achieve this. The New Testament also tells us of joy through pain; the highest and most enduring joy men and women can know.

Take your share of suffering . . . *For the Gospel.* There is the Gospel according to Matthew, and according to Mark, and to Luke, and there is the Gospel according to *you,* and to you, and to me. And the numbers of people who will read the Gospel according to Matthew, and Mark, and Luke, and John are very largely dependent upon the numbers of people that see in the Gospel according to you and me something persuasive. Only as we incarnate the loving hands of Christ are people likely to be attracted to the Gospel and believe it. They are likely to be attracted if we are the kind of persons who take more than our share of suffering.

And finally, "Take your share of suffering . . . for the Gospel. . . . *In the Power of God.*"

We in America are a self-reliant people and are proud of it. We should be. But too often we try to carry our share of suffering in our own strength as described in the poem, "Invictus" which finally finishes:

> I am the master of my fate
> I am the captain of my soul.

That sounds good, doesn't it? It is better than sniveling self-pity. But it won't work. It is like Atlas trying to bear the world on his back. He breaks under it. Anyone who tries to carry his burden alone will become bitter, and hard, and disillusioned before he gets through.

St. Paul can help us here. Paul, you remember, had a thorn in the flesh. We are told that this thorn was epilepsy, and when he was preaching as I am doing tonight, sometimes he would be caught by a fit and be thrown to the earth, would grovel in the sand, froth at the mouth, be humiliated and everybody embarrassed. He never knew when it was going to take hold of him, and he prayed earnestly that God would remove this thorn in his flesh; but God never did. God answered Paul's prayer saying, "My grace will be sufficient." That is, He said to Paul, "I will not take it from you but I will give you the strength to bear it."

I know that most of you have a thorn in the flesh, both the people who sit here and the people who listen over the radio. Because I know

> If every man's internal care
> Were written on his brow,
> How many would our pity share
> Who have our envy now!

Have you learned to carry your thorn in the power of God?

Paul, as an old man, comes to the end of his life and gives us his valedictory. He says, "I have fought a good fight and have been kept by the faith and I rejoice." In what does he rejoice? One might expect him to rejoice in his victories, in his escape from the sea, or from being stoned, or in the converts he has won, the churches he has founded, but rather he says, "I rejoice in my infirmities." Is the man crazy? No, he is just old and wise. He looks back over his life and he realizes that he began his ministry as one who was not sympathetic, who was not kindly in his judgments. He sees that this thorn in the flesh, which broke his pride, also made his spirit gentle, kindly, humble and gracious. He saw it was the very thorn in the flesh that he took to God which made his life effective. We should learn that suffering taken to God can be turned by Him into an asset and be fruitful for the Kingdom's purposes.

Now, finally, we, America as a nation, tend to carry our burdens in our own strength. We have remolded our environment. We have whipped everybody who has stood in our way. Our tendency has therefore been to say with cocksure confidence, we will build our own Kingdom of God. With our scientific education we will banish ignorance. With our scientific medicine we will banish disease. With our industrial know-how we will banish poverty around the world. We would build a Kingdom of God on our own specifications and bow God out of His universe with thanks for His provisional services.

We are not the first people that have taken this attitude. Those of us who have traveled around the Mediterranean know that all about its shores there protrude from the drifting sands mute symbols of a greatness now gone. Fingers of beautiful pillars and lovely symmetrical arches, evidence of great civilizations that once were and now are dead. Why?

> Voices are crying from the dust of Tyre,
> From Baalbec and the stones of Babylon:
> "We raised our pillars upon self-desire,
> And perished from the large gaze of the sun."

And it could be so here—it will be so here unless we learn there is no favoritism in God's moral universe. That except "the *Lord* build the house we labor in vain that build it; except the *Lord* watch the city, the watchman watcheth but in vain." Righteousness exalts any nation in any century and sin is a reproach to any people.

In traveling around the world and seeing the other countries of the earth, I have come to love my own nation with a passionate gratitude I never knew before. I believe that God wants to use this great land of ours to lead the world to peace and brotherhood. But if He is to use us we must be a purified and a revived and a refined and a more righteous and a more moral nation than we are now.

We must realistically face the facts which are to be found in our world. First, we must realize that we are in a time of tension which is not like a football game which we can watch and then go home and forget about. The tension is going to last five, or ten, or fifteen, or perhaps twenty years. In such a situation the religious peoples, the two groups of the Hebrew-Christian tradition, must continue to remind the world that an all-out atomic war will not solve our problems. We may have such a war but there will be more problems at the end for those who live through it, than we have now.

Second, that while we must be militarily strong we must not permit ourselves to become military *minded*. It is my conviction that America should never have Universal Military Training. This is the road down which Germany went and Russia is going.

Third, the Church must forever preach the Gospel which is both judgment and mercy. Judgment that we may not become Pharisaical, thanking God that we are not like other people but rather penitent, like the Publican, who confesses his sin. The Church must preach with glory and joy—mercy; the presence of the living Christ who knocks on the door of our hearts and if we open who comes into our lives bringing forgiveness, peace, wisdom and strength by his indwelling presence.

Someone asked me recently whether I thought the walls of our civilization were tumbling down, if this inevitably was the end for Western civilization. This is, at least, a part of the answer. If we, in the United States of America, see in the upthrust of the billion, six hundred million people in the world who never have enough to eat, who oscillate between hunger and sleep, who do not have adequate medicine, or adequate education; if we see in their upthrust and desire for something better for their children as something in itself bad; if we dub it communism, if we try to build a dam across it because we feel it may threaten our high standard of living, then I believe our civilization is doomed; for that, in my judgment, is the wave of the future—the urge of something better on the part of the depressed—and it will go over and around any dam human minds can envision and hands build.

But if the American people can see in this upthrust an urge for something better for their children and for their family—the same urge that brought our forefathers across oceans and mountains and rivers to this glorious land of ours; if we can see it as something that is good, something that is God-given, something that Christ through the foreign missionary efforts or our churches has nourished, and put ourselves at the head of it, lead it and guide it in wholesome directions, then I believe our civilization is not doomed but that the best days it has ever seen lie ahead of us.

So I close as I began with the invitation and admonition, "Take your share of suffering . . . for the Gospel . . . in the power of God."

# 18

## Again Pioneers

### By PAUL M. ROBINSON

IF I COULD CHOOSE ANY PERIOD IN HISTORY IN WHICH TO LIVE,
I would choose to live now. Not because these are easy times, for
they are not. Our world is filled with strange paradoxes. This is
an era of plenty and of want, war and peace, strength without
security, advancement without progress. In all of history there
has never been a time when we were so materially united across
the world as today. You can travel in almost any part of the
world and you will find evidences of what we call "Western culture" or "Western civilization" which is fast becoming the standard for the world. The twin miracles of radio and transportation have brought the world together into a very close neighborhood. And yet, paradoxically enough, never have we been so
divided spiritually, for the world is torn asunder tonight by different ideologies and therefore we have crisis, for whenever you
have material unity and spiritual disunity, you will invariably
have crisis. No, these are not easy times in which to live and these
are not times of your choosing. But by the accident of birth, you
are called upon by destiny to write one of the most interesting

*Paul M. Robinson is president of Bethany Biblical Seminary,
Chicago.*

and one of the most significant chapters in human history, and I envy you.

Now I don't want to deceive you into thinking that these times are going to be easier than they are. Our fathers thought that they could make a better world by simply saying often enough, "Every day, in every way, we are getting better and better." But they found it didn't work. And our generation has learned what it means to be tricked by a false kind of optimism. I am reminded of the Indiana bishop who, living out in a rural area not far from a big city, had a few chickens. But he was disturbed, because every morning at two o'clock one of his prize roosters would crow, heralding the dawn of the day. He couldn't understand why this usually reliable bird would always awaken him at this hour in the morning, so one night he decided to stay up and see what happened. He discovered that the last trolley car from Indianapolis passed his home at just two o'clock and the rooster saw the headlight on the trolley car and thought it was the sun, so he crowed heralding the dawn of a new day. Now I think sometimes that we are guilty of just heralding every passing headlight as the dawn of a new day, when actually our time is dark and difficult and we should realize that we are casting our lot in dangerous places.

Harvard University celebrated its 300th anniversary a few years ago and on that day the freshmen of Harvard paraded down the streets of Cambridge with a banner. What do you suppose they had on it? "This University has waited 300 years for us." Isn't that just like freshmen? But they were exactly right. I'd like to say to you tonight, my young friends, "Our world has been waiting two thousand years for you."

In his great monumental work, *The Epic of America,* James Truslow Adams says that one of the things that have made this a great nation is the fact that we've always had a frontier, and whenever life was difficult in one place, all we needed to do was to pull up our stakes and move westward to conquer a new territory, stake out a new claim, and begin life over again. You are familiar with the progress of our westward migration. Several years ago I was traveling in the State of Nebraska and I came to a little wide place in the road with a couple of houses on each side which I was told was called "Frontier's End." There was a time, you see, when this was on the edge of the frontier. Now, of course, civilization has pressed far beyond that point, until at last it has gone to the sea. There are no more frontiers in America. So, the frontiers all over the world have one by one disappeared until the great historian says, "The trouble with our world today is that we have no more frontiers. Our world frontiers are gone." I wonder if they are.

The geographical frontiers, of course, are gone, but I wonder if our generation has not brought to light the new and real frontiers of this last half of the twentieth century. Let me illustrate what I mean with a story which I learned from Muriel Lester which haunts my mind. She said that shortly before the release of atomic energy upon the world, two Britishers, a scientist and a minister, were sitting in a London club. They were discussing atomic energy, and the British scientist said, "We do not yet know the extent of the power in this new discovery, but if it is as powerful as I think it is, I give civilization just ten years to survive." And then he paused and added, "Unless"—turning to his friend the clergyman—"Unless you and the other Christian people of the world are able to create spiritual foundations which can sustain an atomic world." I say that story haunts me because more than half of the ten years are gone. You see, he was pointing out that the real frontiers of this time are in the realm of the spirit.

In the fifteenth, sixteenth and seventeenth centuries, the frontiers of the world were *geographical*. It was the era of the explorers, Columbus, Magellan, the trading companies. One by one they conquered the new territories and colonized them. In the eighteenth century the frontiers were in the area of *government*. This was the period in which our great democracies were being forged on the anvil of human rights, and the freedom and liberties which we so cherish were born. The nineteenth century frontiers were *industrial*. Our economy was expanding. We underwent new industrial revolutions which completely changed the life of every nation. We must admit that the frontiers in the first half of this twentieth century were certainly in the realm of *science*. Think, if you will, at the marvelous inventions which have come into the world during the first half of this twentieth century and how life has been completely changed because of them. If all of this be true, surely the great frontier in this last half of the twentieth century is in the area of *human relations*. Now, you see, the great problem which is facing us and all mankind is simply, Can we learn to live together in a world like this? Unless we solve this problem, my young friends, there will be no other problem.

Among the papers of the late F. Scott Fitzgerald, the playwright, was the plot for a play which he never wrote. It goes something like this. Five people, members of the same family who lived in widely separated parts of the world, inherited a house if they would come and live in it together. Isn't that a marvelous plot for a play? Do you realize that this is the drama of the next half century? We, who live in widely separated parts of the world, and some of us here together tonight, must live in this same world together peacefully if any of us are to survive.

Back in the days of the one-room country school, which I am sure you 4-H Club people cannot remember, but which some of us older folks can, we didn't worry too much about fire drills, because there was just about one window for every child and in the case of any emergency, it was everybody out the nearest window. But in our lovely consolidated schools today that plan wouldn't work at all. We teach our children how to evacuate a building in a few seconds in an orderly fashion with fire drills. We know that the safety of every child depends upon his co-opera-tion. If any one child doesn't want to co-operate, he not only endangers his own life, but the lives of all of the other children. Our mutual safety depends upon the co-operation of all of us. What a parable of the world in which we live. Our mutual safety depends upon the co-operation of all of us, and unless from every nation we are able to bring the best of our culture, the best of our traditions, and learn how to live together, none of us will have a world in which to live. So, you see, the great frontiers of your generation are in the area of human relations and once again, whether you like it or not, *you are the pioneers.*

Pioneering is never easy, of course, but there is a certain amount of challenge in it, for as the Indies challenged Columbus, so today you the youth of America are challenged to a world without war. As these early explorers set out to discover new lands, so you must set out to discover a new spirit—a spirit which can eventually bring peace to the world.

We like to brag a little about our forefathers who had the hardiness and the courage to move out from comfortable areas into new and untried ways. We like to think about the Pilgrims who braved the dangers of the North Atlantic and came to these shores without any material possessions, simply because they wanted to establish themselves in a free land where they could have a new way of life. And some of you, I dare say, are the descendants of these hardy pioneers who braved the western plains, facing all manner of hardships, because intangible spiritual liberties were of greater value to them than any temporal, physi-cal benefits.

The pioneering in this half of the twentieth century will be no less difficult, for we must conquer the wilderness of the human heart which is the most difficult frontier to subdue. In the last analysis, I think, all the problems of the world come back to the problems of the individual. We speak of our vexing social and economic and political problems when actually these are but the extension of individual weaknesses. Our world problems are but personal problems multiplied, so that in the last analysis the real difficulty is in man himself—not in our institutions. Institutions in themselves do not succeed or fail. It is people that succeed or fail. An institution is only as strong as the human personality which establishes it. Your church is just as strong as its members. Your school is just as good as the people in it. The club to which you belong is just as succesful as the members are successful. You can have the most beautiful blueprint, but unless the builders will follow it, it can lead to nothing worth while.

I wandered through the buildings of the old League of Nations in Geneva. I could almost see the ghost of Woodrow Wilson there, with many others who had dreamed the League into ex- istence. I remembered how many of us in America weren't sure that we wanted to co-operate with the people in other lands. Then I thought of what Sir Winston Churchill once said, "The League of Nations might have succeeded, if the peoples of the world had wanted it to succeed." The fault did not lie with the League of Nations; the fault lay with the people of the world who were not ready yet for this kind of international co-operation. In- stitutions in themselves do not succeed or fail, only people. And you are called upon, you see, to pioneer in this area of human rela- tions which deals with the problem of man. That's why your task is going to be so difficult. Laying out plans and objectives is not enough. You've got to get to the root of the problem which is human nature. You are called upon to blaze new trails and to establish new social patterns—again pioneers.

During the days of the First World War my family lived in Iowa, and I still remember in my childhood some of the mud roads we had to use. Now, will you people from Iowa please forgive me. I know you have most beautiful highways there now, but back in those days we had mud roads. In these mud roads there were ruts, worn by the wheels of traffic, and once you got down in this rut, you couldn't get out of it. You had to stay there. I remember seeing a sign over one of them which read, "CHOOSE YOUR RUT WELL, YOU'LL BE IN IT FOR THE NEXT TWENTY MILES." That was literally true. Now, my young friends, do you know what's happened in our world? There have been certain ruts established by the tread of social and economic vehicles which have been made deeper and deeper and deeper across the years. Society has just fallen into these ruts and nobody has yet had the courage to try to get out of them. The tragedy is this: once you get into a rut, you are not free to choose your destination. You go where the rut takes you.

At the close of the First World War, we were given an opportunity to establish new patterns of international co-operation. We made only feeble efforts, for soon we discovered that that kind of pioneering was difficult. So we soon slipped back into the old ruts of nationalism and selfishness, and it wasn't long until those old ruts had taken us to the same tragic destination. Now after we have passed through a more terrible war, once again we are given the opportunity to establish some new ruts of international co-operation across the face of humanity. There are some courageous souls among us with the courage of pioneers who have said, "We will not slip back into the old ways, ours will be a new world of understanding and peace." But the way of understanding is narrow and demanding, and little by little I can feel our nation slipping back into the comfortable ways of isolationism, nationalism and selfishness which says we must look out for ourselves, we can't be concerned with all the rest of the world, forgetting, you see, that we are all in the schoolhouse together.

The big question facing your generation is, "Will you have the courage to blaze new trails across our world, establishing new social patterns that will lead to world peace and brotherhood?" Now it's not going to be easy to do that. It always takes courage to establish new patterns. For example, what do you think of when I say "patriotism"? Oh, I know what comes to some of our minds—a parade on Armistice Day or on the Fourth of July with somebody carrying a flag. That's one kind of patriotism. But I wonder when some of us will discover that it takes as much real patriotism to *live* for our country as to *die* for her?

The summer before last I met with a group of young people in Germany. They came from twenty different nations. We were sitting amid the ruins of the most devastating bombing the world has ever seen. All around us were jutting half-destroyed buildings reminding us of man's inhumanity to man. What were these young people doing there? Dropping more bombs? No, they said the world has had enough of that, they had come to establish some new patterns. They were attending an international work camp where they were paying for the privilege of helping to rehabilitate some of these bombed-out communities among a people who just a few years ago were called our enemies. These young people are taking international relations into their own hands. They are going into these bombed-out areas and building homes for people, re-establishing schools and churches, getting to know the people who formerly hated them. The best good will I have seen abroad in Europe and in the Middle East has been created not by our diplomats but by Christian people who have had the courage to live a genuine spirit of understanding. Here are the pioneers of this last half of the twentieth century—pioneering in the area of understanding of human relations. I wonder if you young people have the courage to do that?

One of the things which disturb me is the fact that we are sending so many of our fine young men and women into the world of natural or physical science, and so few into the area of human relations, which is the most exacting science in our world today. We need the very best minds in America to attack this problem of understanding among peoples and nations.

Let me take another area. The Declaration of Independence says that each person is endowed by his Creator with certain inalienable rights such as life, liberty and the pursuit of happiness. Yet, we know that there are certain situations within our nation which make those statements almost a mockery. Out in California, according to Father Keller's remarkable book, *You Can Change the World,* there was a Negro boy who was earning his money to go through college by working at a filling station. But there were some of the people in the community who objected to being served by a Negro. They threatened to take their business elsewhere unless his employer did something about it. So the employer, not wishing to lose any of his customers, decided that the only thing to do was to let the young man go. Now, I suppose there were a good many people in that community who might have clucked their tongues and said, "Isn't it too bad? Somebody ought to do something about it." But one lady who had no responsibility at all for the situation decided that there was something she could do. She went to the employer and said, "How many customers do you think you would lose if you retained this man?" He replied, "Oh, I suppose maybe eighteen or twenty." She said, "If I get you twenty new customers, will you keep him?" And he answered, "I guess I would." She did better; she got him twenty-five new customers. Now, that's creative thinking. Here was a woman who dared to be a pioneer. I wonder if you've got the courage to establish some new social patterns in a world filled with such prejudice?

I remember a young man who lived about two thousand years ago. He lived far beyond his time. Even in his own day he saw that the real frontiers in the world were not geographical, they were in the human heart, in the spirit of man. So he dared to set himself to the task of changing the world by changing men's lives. He had a rough time of it. He was finally nailed to a cross and put to death. But he discovered that if you want to save your life, you've got to lose it, and that the greatest joy in the world comes from giving yourself to something that's bigger than you are.

You, my young friends, are again pioneers in this your generation. I wonder if you have his courage, if you will follow in his train? That's what it means to be a Christian.

Do you remember those stirring words of Walt Whitman, in his poem "O Pioneers"? They might have been written for you so clearly do they sound the summons to spiritual adventure for your time:

> For we cannot tarry here,
> We must march my darlings, we must bear the brunt of danger,
> We the youthful sinewy races, all the rest on us depend,
> Pioneers! O pioneers!

>             .    .    .

> Have the elder races halted?
> Do they droop and end their lesson, wearied over there beyond
>     the seas
> We take up the task eternal, and the burden and the lesson,
> Pioneers! O pioneers!

>             .    .    .

> Till with sound of trumpet,
> Far, far off the daybreak call—hark! how loud and clear
>     I hear it wind,
> Swift! to the head of the army!—swift! spring to your places,
> Pioneers! O pioneers!

# 19

## The Perils of the Christian Life

### By PAUL E. SCHERER

I WANT TO TALK TO YOU TONIGHT ABOUT THE PERILS OF THE
Christian life. It's something we don't often talk about. We
don't like to think about them. Jacob had to face them. He
dreamed of a ladder set up on earth, reaching to heaven, and
saw the angels of God ascending and descending on it, and heard
a voice saying, "I am the Lord God of thy father Abraham, the
God of Isaac. Behold, I will be with thee and will not leave thee
until I have done that which I have spoken to thee of." That
doesn't say anything about peril, does it? It's a very gracious
promise. And yet Jacob had to run a whole gamut of perils before ever God could make that promise true. We don't like to
think about them, because we want to get to the promise before
we ever deal with the perils. We are restless that way.

The first peril Jacob had to face, and we've got to face it too,
is the peril of what I'm going to call *the lost aim*. The very first
word he spoke on waking up was, "Surely the Lord is in this
place, and I knew it not." There wasn't any particular reason
why he should have known it. He wasn't used to discerning the
presence of God anywhere in his life. He was far too busy with

*Paul E. Scherer is professor of homiletics at Union Theological
Seminary, New York City.*

other things. Back home, way down in the south, he'd been busy about his brother's birthright. He'd stolen it, in fact, and had had to get away in a hurry. This dream along the road was just a kind of interruption, nothing more than that. It soon faded from his memory. It was hardly over before he began bargaining with God. "If God will bring me back, and give me food to eat, and raiment to wear, and see that I arrive safely at my father's house, he shall be my God, and I will give him a tenth of all I have." There's no record anywhere of that tenth.

So he was off to his uncle Laban's, and there it was Rachel he was after, not God, just as soon as he laid eyes on her! After seven years of hard labor, he got her older sister Leah. She wasn't so attractive. When he pledged seven more years, Rachel was thrown in. Meanwhile, he worked out a very profitable bargain for himself in the matter of his uncle's herds. He got control of a good many of them. Until one day he was on the way back to his father's house, still running, and this time from Laban! No, he hadn't had much time to find out anything about God. He was too busy.

Now you'll never really get the pathos of that story, or the conscious irony with which it is written, until you remember that in the Bible it's the knowledge of God which gives life meaning. That, and nothing else. Without it, life is just a jumble, a meaningless, futile, pointless jumble. And that's precisely what this cheating two-timer, this runaway, was making out of it, because he didn't know what the knowledge of God meant. I'm not so sure we do.

Do you realize that the Bible does not primarily invite us to any knowledge about God? I think sometimes we lose our aim because we forget that. We are not invited either to any misting over of the eyes at the thought of how good God has been to us. Nor are we invited to the swallowing whole of some pious notion that sticks in our throats. To none of that. And we'd better be clear about it. There was a very reputable author not long ago in a reputable religious journal who had this to say: "Jesus and His disciples accepted the idea of the supremacy of God without question." As if the supremacy of God were an idea that we had to accept without question, in an age which is doing its very level best to deny and cancel God's supremacy, and making a good job of it! Where was the supremacy of God when soldiers drove great spikes through Jesus' hands and feet? We've got to think a bit more deeply before we use such phrases. Where was that supremacy when *you* lost everything you had, when somebody you loved died long before the time, or so *you* thought. It's hardly less than criminal to keep suggesting to us that we've got to begin listening to God's good news by rubbing our eyes like Alice in Wonderland, and believing something which manifestly is not so as it stands. The Queen said to Alice when she seemed bewildered, "Why, nothing is easier than believing something that isn't so. All you need is a little practice. I quite often believe what isn't so half a dozen times before breakfast. Every morning I practice." It won't do. We are invited to meet God.

That's what the Gospel is about. Nothing else. And that's why the Bible reads to us like a strange book. Because it isn't an empty world, that world of the Bible, like our world. It's a world that's filled with God. You keep running into this infinite mind, keep stumbling upon the sound of that yearning, eternal heart. If you want to try an experiment, take any page and strip it of God, as we strip our lives, down to the bone, with that infinite mind away somewhere, and that eternal heart just a grand perhaps. And all of a sudden you'll be right back in the world that you know all too well, where a sower sowing his seed is just a sower sowing his seed, nothing more than that, where laborers stand idle in the market place, and where nothing is a parable because God hasn't anything to do with any of it, and the whole place is stale, flat and unprofitable, and makes you sick.

The difference between us and these more stalwart souls of the Bible was simply this: that when they looked at the world they saw Him, when they listened to the Babel of the world's voices they heard His voice. Everywhere in their days there was something God wanted them to do, and they got their fingers on it, and carried it through, and laid it down with a happy sigh at night. No wonder their world was full of songs. Would you like to swap your world for theirs? Well, you can, whenever you like.

"Surely the Lord is in this place, and I knew it not." Maybe that could say something to you about these hours you have at the Sunday Evening Club. If nobody is acting here but those of us who are here on the platform, then you do quite well to ask yourselves if the show was interesting. But if God is acting here, then that's the wrong question. Then you've got to ask if He has any word for your soul. Then that finite self of yours, in all its insignificance, has come up before the Infinite. Then the pollution of your life is at this moment come up before the Holy. Then you, the creature, in all your dependence, have in this instant come up before God, the Creator. You are now beyond the realm of ideas and of things. You have met God. That's what Christianity is about, nothing else, and nothing less.

There is another peril: the peril of the *complacent self*. Suddenly Jacob realized that in the presence of God he wasn't comfortable. He understood that he'd forgotten what life was about. He'd been all ready to settle down, quite content with himself, with things as they were, in the way he managed his own business, in the way he treated other people. Now suddenly he was disturbed, and he trembled and was afraid, and said, "How dreadful is this place." That the Lord was there wasn't just the most pleasant idea that could have occurred to him. "This is none other but the house of God."

I suppose nobody is quite so likely to turn complacent as those of us who call ourselves Christians, just because we've grown used to being what we are. We've listened to sermons preached about God, we've read a few books about Him, we talk about Him occasionally, and now and then recommend Him very, very highly. We can even explain the mysteries of His dealings, particularly when somebody else is hurt by them. We can give you definitions and answers to your questions, and tell you precisely what's wrong with you the minute you ask us, and advise you as to just what you ought to do. All of which I say by way of gentle satire. And I'm rather well pleased with it. How well pleased are you with yourself because you suspected that I was well pleased with myself? That's how subtle complacency really is!

Did you ever notice the old revival hymns? They come pretty near it.

> On Christ the solid Rock I stand.
> All other ground is sinking sand.

That's splendid, until you begin shaking hands with your own virtue. Then it isn't so *splendid*. You catch the sound of this complacency in the Gospels over and over again—not often on the lips of bad people, but on the lips of good people. The dear soul who clasped her hands when she saw Jesus acting so gallantly in the midst of his enemies, and cried out, "Blessed is the womb that bare thee." She didn't see anything wrong with that. All she meant to say was, "How happy Your mother must be to have a Son like You." That's what it meant, really. And Jesus turned on her with a flash and said, "No, no, not that. Blessed are they that hear the word of God, and keep it." A man ran up to him one day and said, "Lord, I will follow thee whithersoever thou goest," and Jesus said, "The foxes have holes, and the birds of the air have nests, and the Son of man hath not where to lay his head." There was a guest at a dinner. He exclaimed, "How splendid it will be to sit down in the kingdom of God at the last!" And Jesus turned to him and asked, in effect, "Are you sure you'll be there?" Always he met them with that quick recoil. Why? Because something was there which had made haste too quickly. That's what complacency is. Some sanctification that's premature, that's an aeon or two ahead of schedule. Complacency is that state of the soul which in fancy deems itself a great deal better than it is in fact. And the eyes of God are on it. "How dreadful is this place."

Jesus told a parable once about a king who gave a wedding feast for his son, and when the guests were all assembled the king came in to see them, looked around a moment, and went over to a man who had not on a wedding garment, and said to him, "Friend, how camest thou in hither?" And the man was speechless, because he knew he didn't have to come that way. He just chose to, that's all. Maybe it means that he'd come for the wrong reason. Does that get close to you? He'd come because somebody had told him there was a great deal to be had by coming. As in our case tonight, somebody may have said to you, "Well, there's much to be had, really. Perhaps a faith that can move mountains of inferiority and guilt. Perhaps a religion that can undergird the democratic way of life." That man at the wedding feast had on the same old workaday clothes that all of us wear when we go abroad to look out for Number One, and it wouldn't do. The king came in to see the guests, and said, "Bind him hand and foot, and take him away." Sir Winston Churchill once said, in his whimsical fashion, that we were quite chock-a-block with futile, panic fears. Said he, "A tiny mouse enters the room, and all the mighty potentates tremble." Shall Almighty God enter the room, and nobody turn a hair? "The king came in to see the guests."

Maybe the guest was there too cheaply. Is there anybody here tonight all wrapped about with his own comfortable adventures

into righteousness? Quite sure he'll pass muster under those
steady eyes? Not much concerned about how things are with
him? Nothing inside that's grim and tense, holding on with its
fingertips to something that's farther than he can reach, and
harder than he can do? And always that steady scrutiny! You
know, I'm really amazed to think how few of our hymns ever say
anything about it. You're going to sing a hymn at the close of
this service that doesn't say a thing about it, and I want you, as
you sing it, to remember those steady eyes, before you dare fill
your lungs and tell God how all right everything is, when He
comes into the room.

I read with a cold chill the other day of a wounded soldier,
looking up at a visitor in the hospital who had said, meaning
well, "I'm sorry you lost your leg"—and answering bravely, "I
didn't lose it. I traded it in for an easy conscience." But an easy
conscience is the only thing in this world that we have no right to,
when God is around! No right at all! It's an awful and a lonely
meeting when you accept the invitation that the Bible holds out
to you. It's an invitation to meet God!

Well then, are we ready for the promise now? Not quite. From
the peril of the lost aim through the peril of the complacent self,
Jacob came at last to what I'm going to call the peril of the *far
horizon*. "This is the gate of heaven." Years were to pass before
he was to find out how much it was going to cost him to enter
that gate. He didn't find out until he was on his way back to his
father's house. And there by night an angel met him; met him
on the banks of the river Jabbok, that deep ravine; met him and
wrestled with him. When the angel saw that he did not prevail,
he touched Jacob's thigh, and Jacob's thigh was out of joint.
And the angel said, "Let me go, because the day breaketh." And
Jacob answered, "I will not let thee go, except thou bless me."
Something by now was happening to the man. As he crossed the
river, the sun rose upon him, and he halted upon his thigh. It

was the dawn of the new life, but he had to limp into it. That's the risk all of us run.

I don't know what you make of this story. Maybe it's legend. Maybe it's saga. But I do know that it's the epic of all this shadowed human life of ours, where we have to deal over and over again with the presence of God, with His steady scrutiny, and at the last and at the worst, with His ruthless love that will not let us go on as we are, that will hurt us before it will let us go on. There is something terrifying about the experience when it's real, when at the last, things have gone on long enough, and God has to take a hand Himself, when the wrestling is no longer with an uneasy conscience, but with the very God who has made the conscience uneasy!

The disconcerting thing about God is that in this drama of human life He is billed as a friend, and for the first two chapters of Genesis He acts like it—two whole chapters. Then in the third, because we are what we are, He begins to behave for all the world as if He were a foe. Riffle the pages of the Bible, and you'll be amazed that you ever missed it. All along He's standing over against His people. See how contrary the prophets are, Isaiah, Jeremiah. Whenever the majority think they have things well in hand, they go over and speak for His Majesty's loyal opposition. When everybody says "Yes," they say "No." And you never do understand them until you yourself come to grips with this God who will at the last come to grips with you.

It's tragic, the way this culture in which we live has taught us to think constantly of our God as if He were a great ally. We sing "God Bless America." Did you ever think of the problem He has on His hands when He tries to answer that prayer? Did it ever occur to you that you might not like His answer? The Jews didn't. In our own individual lives we've grown so used to thinking of a benign and beneficent Providence, that we're quite sure, thanks to Him, everything will turn out all right. All you have to do is to make up your mind where you're going, and carry the Ark of God along. "Take Jesus with you." Then something happens that doesn't fit your idea of what God ought to do, and you begin to understand that before He can ever be a Friend He has to be the great Antagonist.

This is the peril of the far horizon: Jacob in danger, not from Esau his brother, but from the angel that met him on the banks of the river Jabbok. Deadly peril. Matters had come to a crisis now, and there was no exit. He held out great handfuls of the stuff that he had gathered together, trying to bribe Esau into friendship, sent one company ahead of another, saying, "This is a present for my lord, and thy servant cometh on behind." Only to find that Esau was quite willing to receive him without any of that. Jacob was so relieved that he gave Esau half his goods before he could catch himself. But that wasn't the peril at all. The peril now was God. Love was rolling up its sleeves.

Way back in the days of the first Elizabeth in England, men used to swear by God's wounds. They meant the wounds God got in Jesus of Nazareth. Can we not remember that there are wounds that God gives, and that often we are hurt by them, because He wants to heal us? The children of Israel in the wilderness muttered to themselves, "Would God we had died in Egypt, when we sat by the fleshpots"; but they didn't. They left their bones in the desert. They died of the wounds God gave them. Here's a man though, who is on the road to being saved by those wounds. He's crying out, "O would God that I had died for thee, Absalom, my son, my son!" That's David, feeling the burden of life at its heaviest, and wanting to get under it still further, to see if he could lift it. And over in the New Testament is another —Paul, standing before Festus and Agrippa in chains, "Would God ye were all as I am, save these bonds." God had saved him by the wounds He gave. And the deepest of all is this: there was One who bore it for our redemption. "Not my will, but Thine, be done."

"As he passed over Penuel, the sun rose upon him, and he halted upon his thigh."

O God, Thou who art untamed and perilous, who dost deal in every form of danger, and many modes of death, strip us of our pretensions and our vanities, expose to the strong his weakness, and to the wise his folly, but set in our hearts an unconquerable hope, and in Thine own way fulfill it, through Jesus Christ, our Lord. Amen.

# 20

# World Neighbors

## By SAMUEL M. SHOEMAKER

THE CHRISTIAN RELIGION BEGAN WHEN GOD SENT HIS SON INTO the world to be the Friend and Saviour of mankind. Our first duty, therefore, is always to worship and serve and obey God, the God whom we know in Jesus Christ. To those who would put human kindness above our duty to God, we must always say, "Yes, but Christ didn't put it that way. He did put the duty to God first and the duty to the neighbor next." It is a danger we often run by thinking that we can be Christians because we are kind.

But there's another danger, and that is the danger of pursuing a merely personal faith in God, affirming often our belief in the eternal verities of Christianity through the Creed, drawing on God for help through prayer and through the Sacraments and through worship, while forgetting that this is all both an end in itself, because God is Himself an end, the great End, the most important fact in all the universe hence the word "worship," (which means really "worthship"), and also is the first step in the right kind of service to man.

The moment Isaiah had seen his vision of God, high and lifted

*Samuel M. Shoemaker is pastor of Calvary Episcopal Church, Pittsburgh.*

199

up, and realized his sin and had been purged of it, he heard Somebody saying, "Whom shall I send, and who will go for us?" Send where? Go to whom? Go to those other people who have not seen God, high and lifted up nor anywhere else, nor known Him. Go to those in need. Go to share with others the blessings that you yourself enjoy. That's the voice which all who come anywhere near to God hear, the voice of God saying, "Go."

Some years ago at an important juncture in my life I conferred with one of the great Christian leaders of this day who has many times spoken on this platform, and I asked him what he thought was essential, and without a hesitation he said to me, "Two things are essential: the great world movement of the Church, and the everlasting emphasis upon the individual." I think that was wisdom. Your religion and mine ought to be an ellipse around two foci. Those two foci are the world and the individual. After we have renewed our worship of God we ought to turn back at once and instinctively to persons who need us, and to thinking about the winning of the world for Christ. To think of religion as consisting purely in private, personal religious practice can be and sometimes is absolutely selfish. The world is full of nominal Christians whom neither Malenkov nor Satan has the least fear of. They're preoccupied with their own little personal concerns, parochial concerns, and of course the devil and communism are playing for much bigger stakes. They're playing for the world, and so is the Lord Jesus Christ, and so are the people who really follow him.

Now when it comes to the world movement of the Church, it is not very many years since the vast underprivileged part of the world was like a huge vacuum. There they lay, huge numbers of Chinese, Japanese, Koreans, Malayans, Indians, Iranians, Africans, and many more. They had been there a long time, and we thought they were going to be there a long time more. We could move in with our Christian mission as we were able to raise funds for it, and find the people to go. It was a great enterprise, and a growing one, all through the nineteenth century. We could, in a sense, take our time. The fields were open. Nobody was there to contest them with us.

Now all that is changed. We confront a great and terrible movement. China, for instance, is no longer an open field, waiting for some of us to come and cultivate it with ideas of faith and of freedom. China, partly by a series of blunders on our part which seem to me to be without defense, was betrayed by the free nations into the hands of the Communists and has slipped behind the Iron Curtain, for nobody knows how long. I love those people. I lived among them for two most important years in my life. As Congressman Walter Judd was pointing out a little while ago, China is the hand, and there are twelve fingers extending off from it, from the Kuriles all around to Iran. Now communism has trained missionaries in those lands, missionaries to stir up trouble, to capitalize on the sore spots, to make much of exploitation and mistakes on the part of the West (and we've had plenty of them), getting little groups together to indoctrinate them, and making Communist converts every hour.

Some of us in our blindness, stupidity and shortsightedness said we "did not believe in foreign missions." Joe Stalin wasn't such a fool. He believed in foreign missions plenty. When you've drunk deep of atheistic materialism, you also hear a voice saying, "Whom shall I send, and who will go for us?" Send where? Go to whom? Go to those starving millions who long to come up in the world and have a decent standard of living! Go to them, and tell them that communism will give them the moon, and they'll believe it. Nothing could be worse than what they have, or rather what they haven't. Communism believes in foreign missions with a vengeance. Many of us Christians sit back in futility and watch the Communists take the world. They're doing it at the rate of a hundred million a year. Tens of millions wait in the balance, wondering whether their best interests lie with the Communists or with the free world.

Now, what's going to turn the scales in the vast part of the world which still is not decided where its interests lie? Will radio broadcasts about how many refrigerators and automobiles we have do it for people who've never seen an automobile or a refrigerator? Will moving pictures of amorous adventures and bathing beauties sent out to countries where women still wear veils? Certainly not. Nor will those who represent American business or government or foundations, whose lives do not match their missions.

Congressman Judd talked recently about having seen an Iranian who told him about government representatives who went out under Point Four or some other government help, and worked at the village level for the first hours of the day, but then in the evening were found at the club or the hotel, dancing with the landlord's daughter, and he said those two things didn't match. He asked, "Whom do your people come out here to live with and work with and serve?" It looks as if we've got to train every American to be an ambassador of freedom and of faith wherever he goes, and tell him he is never off guard. He is being watched by people to see whether he takes seriously our democracy, and the Christianity which stands behind that democracy.

Now above all this welter and confusion, one man has spoken with a plan that seems to some of us inspired. His name is Frank Laubach. He is to me one of the half dozen greatest Christians alive, perhaps of the greatest men alive, from where I sit. He has called for a "war of amazing kindness." He says we've got to go into the underprivileged countries and *do* what communism only *promises* to do. We need to take them modern know-how. They need help in health and in engineering, in agriculture and in education. Dr. Laubach says that if we sent to different parts of the underprivileged world that are still open, a hundred thousand skilled and trained men and women, color blind as to race, with humility and friendliness, with love for God and love for people in their hearts, people who pray, and people who believe in Christ, we would do two things. We would help those people to "come up" as they want to do, and we'd also keep them out of the Communist camp. He says to do that right would cost about two billion dollars. Set that over against the cost of a third world war, and see how inexpensive an operation that would really be.

Dr. Laubach says we've got to do this thing together. Let no one look down his nose at what other people are trying to do. The government is in this with what is now called FOA. Now better personnel is often needed, with more humility, more Christian faith, to approach these people, and perhaps more courtesy and reverence and friendliness. The great foundations are doing a great deal already. Business sends upward of ten thousand people a year to represent them in foreign countries. Those people ought to be briefed about their lives, not about how to sell their product only, for they are ambassadors of the free West, and not just representatives of some individual company. All our service men and women ought to be helped to understand the vastness and cruciality of the enterprise in which they are engaged if they are overseas. It's quite as much diplomatic as it is military, and yet many of them are not sufficiently instructed in what lies behind their military duties, and how important are their contacts with people. Every traveler ought to go, not to please himself, not to see strange sights and to meet unusual people, but to get into the homes and lives, especially of the underprivileged people. That's where the Communists go to get their work done.

Of course, the churches have done something. There's no calculating what has been done by such an institution, for instance, as the Allahabad Agricultural College in India, where Sam Higginbottom was for so many years. I saw that amazing place with my own eyes about thirty years ago, and know what signal service a man like that and his predecessors and successors have done. The tragic thing is, though, that out of some nine thousand and more missionaries in all the non-Roman churches there were, when I got the last count, only eighty-five agricultural missionaries. That is simply not enough. We've sent them out a little at a time as if we had centuries to do it. We haven't got months to do it. We may not even have days. There lies an emergency upon us today, I believe, such as was never confronted by the Christian forces of the world before. Our own, and vast numbers of other men's freedoms is imperiled, and our own survival as well as theirs, dictates that we act, and try to act quickly.

Now, swept with the vision of Dr. Laubach, a little group of us got together out in Columbus, Ohio, in September, 1952, and we founded an organization that's called "World Neighbors." We persuaded Dr. Roy Burkhart, the brilliant minister of the great First Community Church in Columbus, to head that movement, and he has spent himself recklessly in that service, giving for a great many months about three quarters of his time to direct that movement. We also asked later an extraordinary fellow, whose name is John Peters. John Peters was a minister out in Oklahoma, and one Sunday he started to preach an ordinary sermon to his congregation. But after he'd heard about this movement, he just couldn't preach that sermon. He went into his pulpit and he talked to his people about the real issues. Some of his men got behind him. They met on Monday night and raised seven or eight thousand dollars, and set in motion something which was then called "World Assistance." We knew that World Assistance was already doing what World Neighbors was setting out to do, and by a gesture gracious and, I believe, wise, they abandoned their own individuality and came in with us on this whole program of World Neighbors. Now John Peters is giving full time to leading that movement along with Dr. Burkhart.

We invited many representatives of the mission boards and

joint boards to Columbus to guide us in not making mistakes, and in not needlessly overlapping in what was already being done. We wanted to supplement and not supplant what the churches were already doing. We had their cordial endorsement and help.

Now some will say, "Why can't we leave this entirely to the churches?" I should say, going at their present rate, it is extremely difficult for the churches to get there in time. We are often bound by ecclesiastical organizations. We are sometimes bound by red tape. And we've got to act on an emergency basis now. Those who want to give through their churches can do so. We are trying to enlarge on what is already existing. But we must do more, vastly more, than is being done now.

I should also say that I think we have on the whole failed in the churches to make foreign missions seem a significant world force to the average American. He's illiterate and uninformed and ignorant about it. The ordinary American thinks of foreign missions as the concern of a small group of pious and perhaps narrow and self-righteous people. He's wrong, but there he is. Now this movement comes along and puts right under his nose the shocking and indeed terrifying facts of the world situation, and offers him something that he can do about it. It draws him in on what the church has been trying to get him to help to do all along, because now he sees the relation between this work and practical world affairs. If we had believed in foreign missions before we would have done better than we are doing at the present time. The average Protestant gift to foreign missions is less than a dollar and thirty cents per head per annum, and I can't get a haircut and pay a tip in Pittsburgh for a dollar and thirty cents.

Persist in calling this thing just foreign missions and a lot of people are going to turn away, but let the ordinary, practical, hardheaded and very goodhearted American see that this might have something to do with turning the world away from the slavery of communism, and he may be ready to help you to do it. I cannot think of a better way to package our Christian belief, and to get that belief across to those who do not hold it, than by helping our brown and black and yellow neighbors across the sea to find a more abundant life and Christian faith.

Now it's the plan of World Neighbors to establish one hundred and twenty centers in needy spots, and train people there to carry on this work themselves. In as many places as possible this will mean helping already existing agencies to do more work. It meets the need, tries to meet the need at the village level. The first center that we opened up was at a place called Katpadi in the Madras province of southern India. It was chosen because already there was an agricultural institute operating there, whose director is an agricultural graduate of Iowa State. Twenty-five adjacent villages are the immediate areas that are affected. It had to be done through the village people, but it started favorably because of the work that the missionaries had already done. Classes in literacy, sewing, spinning and weaving, improvement in livestock and poultry breeds, rural health, are being conducted, and some small-scale industries have been developed. Volunteers from the villages themselves are given leadership instruction. The team at work there is a typical one, with two Americans and two Indians working together. They are specialists in sanitation, mechanical skills, agriculture and literacy. Our objective is not charity. It is the extension of such self-help as will enable these people increasingly to help themselves. We plan to put a team down to work five years, and then when it's caught on, we can pick that team up and put it down elsewhere, to begin to work another five years. Meantime it goes on under indigenous, local leadership.

Another pilot center is at a place called Anklesvar, on the west coast, north of Bombay. Two young people went out to join the director of a vocational training school there, both of them graduates of Cornell University. The husband is himself an Indian who comes from that region, a trained agronomist. His wife is of Chinese parentage and she's a specialist in nutrition. Nearly twenty near-by villages have been asking for farmers' clinics. Land has been set aside for the demonstration centers. A literacy teacher and specialist in child care and mechanical skills will be added as soon as possible. Now, what can we do?

Well, you might volunteer to go. We need people with a skill, people who know how to do something, and do it well. We need people of faith and of humility. I know of some instances where retired people, who retired rather early, have been greatly used in this way overseas.

Second, we may know of other people like this. Think and pray about such people as that. Talk with your own minister about whether there are people like that in your parish.

Third, some of those people might be able to go on their own expense, or it's possible that some of their neighbors and friends or their churches might be able to take care of some of their expense.

May I also suggest that you read some of the literature on the subject, including the perfectly wonderful story called "Look What This Preacher Started" by Frank and Merle Sinclair which appeared in *The Saturday Evening Post* of December 19, 1953. It tells the whole story of World Neighbors. Perhaps you will feel guided yourself to start a local chapter such as the one here in Chicago. I hope there may be twenty or thirty before we get through with it.

I'd like to read a letter that I had the other day from Dr. John Peters. I asked him for the last information about this. He says, "We're operating on a very modest budget. This year's budget is set at one hundred and fifty thousand. We anticipate we shall certainly raise that amount as the minimum. We now have over twenty chapters, and new ones await organization.

There are groups ranging from ten to eight hundred in number, now supporting World Neighbors in no less than forty-seven cities. We presently have six projects in India, ranging in cost from as little as fifteen hundred to eighteen thousand a year. And we have a project in Egypt and one in the Philippines. We are proceeding to establish two more projects in India and these will average between eight and ten thousand a year. The other projects are being developed in full co-operation with the United Christian Missionary Society of the Disciples of Christ—a commission of Indian and American Christians are presently selecting the site. We've already selected the leader for the World Neighbors extension phase of this subject. His name is Wilbur Hogg, has his master's degree in public health from the University of Southern California, has had previous experience with the American Friends Service Committee in Mexico, and comes to us highly recommended by all who know him. At the last count we had three hundred and nine applicants for overseas work. These include a host of individuals with doctors' degrees, masters' degrees, bachelors' degrees, and a wealth of experience in the basic fields in which we are trying to serve. Among the group is a language competence in twenty-three of the major languages of the world, plus a number of obscure dialects. Altogether we are ready to put a real army into the field. We now have eight projects in operation, two more which will be going within the next few months, with requests for as many as forty others which have come to us from missions and from governments."

Let me add this: I have given my own life to try to extend a deeper kind of personal religion in the life of people, in my church and in other churches. I deeply believe that's where all this starts, and without that we shall not do the other. But I do believe that all that can be very personal, very selfish, very narrow, very ineffectual in the world in which we live, unless we get going on something like World Neighbors. If you know a better way to do it, do that. If you know others who are doing it better than we're doing it, help them instead of us. If you don't know anything better, do get hold of that literature, study it, read it, give us your prayers, your help, your imagination, help us with personnel, help us in any way you can to do this thing which I believe is the most urgent task today on the face of the earth. God help us not to fail Him nor humanity in a day when such a crisis faces us, and such magnificent opportunity!

# 21

# The Drama of Deliverance

## By RALPH W. SOCKMAN

BURIED AT THE HEART OF OUR LORD'S PRAYER IS THE PETITION, "Deliver us from evil." Evil is around us in so many forms, that they almost defy description. Evil in the form of bad environment surrounds us as the sea of troubles encompassed the soul of Hamlet. Evil in the form of unwholesome heredity clings to each new generation as a stubborn winter stifles a struggling spring. Evil in the form of bad desires is in our veins, and sometimes seems to break forth with almost volcanic force. And evil in the form of world bitterness is about us in such terrific threat, that many talk with fear of a third world war. Therefore I know that you're all joining with me tonight when I pray, "Deliver us from evil."

Now, our Bible is a story of a people struggling to be delivered from evil. It's a long unfolding drama of deliverance, and I often think that people would find the Bible far more interesting if they could see it in its long panoramic unfolding story. So many of us, you know, treat the Bible with little interesting paragraphs and favorite passages, but we never see it in its long sweep.

*Ralph W. Sockman is pastor of Christ Church (Methodist), New York City.*

Beginning back there with the patriarchs—Abraham, Isaac and Jacob—in the misty morning of time; then advancing to those days when Joseph went into Egypt, and the slavery engulfed the people of Israel in Egypt: then, when they were led forth by Moses in that mighty exodus; then follow them through the days of the Judges, when they tried to hammer that little tribal group into some form of order; then on to the days of David, who lifted Israel to a new sense of nationhood, and dreamed of a city that he might build; then Solomon, who lifted Israel to a splendor that ever remained the glory of that nation; then, under Solomon, came the taxation, and the burdensome oppression, and the quarrels that divided the nation, and exile began to loom; and out of the tears of the exile in Babylon, they began to dream of a Redeemer, a Messiah who would rescue them; and then, in the fullness of time, came One, whom we, as Christians, call the Messiah, the Redeemer, the One whose birth we are about to celebrate; and then we come on to that glorious Gospel of his work and words, until the Bible ends in the visions of Revelation.

I say, I think if we could see it in that long dramatic sweep, it would become more thrilling to us. And tonight, I'd like to think of the Bible as a drama of deliverance in four acts.

Act I is the stage in which the people thought to deliver themselves by taking it out on somebody else. In those early primitive times, you know, the Israelite did not sit down and say, "O Lord, what have I done? How can I be saved?" He thought that Jehovah dealt with the tribe. And they had a ceremony called the ceremony of atonement, in which they took a goat, and invested that goat with a cloth about its horn. That cloth was supposed to contain the sins and evils of the tribe. Then they took the goat out to the edge of the community, and sent it off into the wilderness, supposedly taking with it the troubles and sins of the people.

That seems like a very superstitious and outmoded custom, doesn't it? But that goat was called the scapegoat, and that's a very modern word. In fact, even today, the first way that people seek to deliver themselves from evil is to find a scapegoat on whom they can put the blame, believing that if they can punish someone, then they will be freed from their ills.

Or suppose that an orgy of crime or corruption broke out in a city. What happens? There's a great hue and cry, perhaps a few people are indicted, convicted, and then, all too often, the public conscience is eased, the people settle back into the same old sins. The conscience has been relieved, but the sins have not been removed.

The world had a scapegoat a few years ago. Back in World War I we said, you know, that if we could get rid of the Kaiser and the Hun, we would have a world safe for democracy and free from war. So we killed thousands of Germans, and lost thousands of men in doing it. And twenty years after, we had a new evil, even worse, we were told—the Nazi peril. And so we had World War II. And again we slaughtered our boys, and slaughtered others, in getting rid of Hitler and the Nazis. And now we're told, only a few years after, that we face a still worse peril in communism.

We've learned, haven't we, that we do not get rid of our sins and evils merely by finding scapegoats? We do not make ourselves good and pure and safe here in America by simply fighting foreign foes abroad. We have to get at something in the human heart.

And sometimes I think, my friends, we're more prone to the scapegoat method today than ever before, for a rather simple reason. Our godly grandfathers used to sit down and look at their sins, in the morning and at night, with family prayer. But we are so prone to begin the day with the first news broadcast in the morning, and close it with the last news broadcast at night, both of which turn our thoughts toward what? Our own sins? Not at all. Toward the sins and evils of others. With the result that we take those precious moments that could be given to self-cleansing and purification, and we make them moments of social condemnation.

Jesus, you know, did just the opposite. Jesus fought the sin, but loved the sinner. We fight the sinner, and keep the sin. The scapegoat method just does not deliver us from evil.

Well, the inspired writers of our Bible woke up to that truth, and they rose to an Act II, a higher stage of the understanding of God. God, you know, is the same, yesterday, today and forever, but we, in our rising understanding, catch new revelations of Him. And the second Act is the stage at which men tried to deliver themselves from evil by taking it out themselves. They said, "We'll no longer blame our fathers for our heredity, and blame our environment. We'll take this responsibility."

Now, that's quite a step upward. When the great moral prophets of the Old Testament said, "No longer shall the people say, 'The fathers have eaten sour grapes, and the children's teeth are set on edge,' " which was the old way of saying the children suffer for their fathers' sins, "Every man that eateth sour grapes, *his* teeth shall be set on edge. Every man shall die for his *own* sins," that was quite a step upward, wasn't it? For you know, it's a childish thing to blame all our evils on our environment and heredity. I do not know how much our conduct is conditioned by heredity and environment. Maybe it's 95 or 98 per cent. Nevertheless, when you find a fellow who gives his heredity and environment as the complete alibi for his misconduct, you have a person in whom there's not much hope of redemption, haven't you? Somewhere, whatever the forces be that play upon us, man must stand up and say, "Here *I* am responsible.

You see, we've begotten a kind of fatalistic mood in this country. A chaplain said to me during the war, "After the war we'll have at least eight or nine million fatalists in America." He said, "The boys I meet on shipboard so often reason like this: 'When the bomb or the bullet comes along with my number on it, it'll get me, so why worry?' Well, when we had tossed our boys into conditions they couldn't control, I didn't take issue very often with them on that point, but you know that's not a Christian philosophy. I said to a young man who talked like that, 'Now wait a minute. Suppose you were on a blacked-out ship at night, and you lighted your cigarette, and the lighting of that cigarette was a signal to a lurking submarine, and it bombed your ship, could you say that that bomb came simply because it had your number on it? Wouldn't you have to admit that your match had something to do with it?' 'Yes,' he said, 'I guess you would.'" Of course. Whatever the forces be that play upon us, there's some place where each one of us must stand up and say, "Here I am responsible. If I've sinned, I'll take the consequences."

Now I say, it's quite a step upward when we reach that stage, but, manly as it may sound to say "We'll deliver ourselves from evil," it just can't be done. I may be beset with a bad habit, and I may be manly enough to say, "I'll check this thing," and I set my will and grit my teeth, but when I set my will I also focus my imagination, and the psychologists tell us that when the will and the imagination are in conflict, the imagination always wins. That's why Alcoholics Anonymous have as their first step, you know, the stage when a man says, "I can't handle this myself," and he calls in a higher help.

So morality is not enough. It's good. But the Hebrew prophets, noble in their ethics, did not have the full secret of deliverance. So the inspired writers of our Bible rose to a still higher conception, Act III.

Act III might be called the stage where they tried to deliver themselves from evil by the strong helping the weak—what we call vicarious suffering and redemption. When the prophet was dreaming of a deliverer for Israel, he rose to that 53rd Chapter of Isaiah. The One who could deliver them would be wounded for our transgressions, and bruised for our iniquities, and the chastisement of our peace would be upon Him, and with His stripes we are healed.

You could paraphrase that, couldn't you, and say it of any good mother. She was bruised for our iniquities, she was wounded for our transgressions. Of course you could. Because you can't run a home without vicarious suffering and help. Mothers, you know, give extra hours and care to little ugly ducklings. Fathers will work their hands to the bone for little crippled boys. There's something in us, that somehow in our family life makes one for all, and all for one. The strong bear the burdens of the weak.

And that's a principle that I think is pretty well spread now in what we call Christian culture. We're far from being Christlike, but at least we've gotten this far, that in our cities and in our lives, the strong do help the weak. The Red Cross reaches out to help the flood sufferers in Holland, or the smog sufferers in London. Your great Community Chests here in Chicago do something each Christmas season that almost goes beyond description.

Of course, that's one of the things we miss in these great cities like New York and Chicago. We don't have quite that sense of responsibility for the person next to us. I was born on a farm in Ohio, and out there I remember that when anything went wrong with some family, the neighbors would chip in and help him. I recall the community chest in the little town where I was. The slogan of that community chest was, "If you don't, who will?" I recall that, because I was in that town to get married, and I said to Mrs. Sockman, "That was put up for my benefit. If you don't, who will?" But in that little town, that was a pretty effective slogan, because you could see your neighbor, you could feel your responsibility, but here in great cities like this, we're lost in the crowd. That's what makes it so difficult to keep up the civic morale and the sense of Christian responsibility in great cities like yours and mine.

Somehow we've got to recapture that. Somehow we must create a new spirit of community in these great metropolitan areas, a community of interest around institutions like this Sunday Evening Club, if you please, around churches, around hospitals, around universities. My church is not a community church, but I'd like to think it's developing a church community, a sense of belonging. That's what we need. That's what Christianity came to give.

I said this morning on the radio that when I was in Calcutta, I saw there on a Sunday afternoon some fifty thousand people milling around some Communist speakers. Who were the members of that crowd? They were the landless, propertyless, ruthless, and in large part jobless people of Calcutta. They had no sense of belonging. They were a fertile soil for the Communist seed. But you get people who feel that they belong, who have a sense of responsibility, who feel others are doing something to help them, and you've got something that's pretty immune to the Communist germ. I've often said, I think the spirit of community is our best defense against communism. That's Act III, where the strong help to bear the burdens of the weak.

There's an Act IV in this drama of deliverance, and I think it was put for me most vividly in that great Negro play, *Green Pastures*. I have great respect for that play, because I heard a New England college president say once that he got more spiritual help from seeing *Green Pastures* than he got from hearing all the preachers that came to his campus that winter. And since I was one of those preachers, I have always remembered the remark.

In that play there's a scene where God is looking down from His heavenly office at the earth. He's talking to the Angel Gabriel, and He says, "What more can I do to save them? I've sent a flood, I've sent plagues, I've sent prophets, and still they

sin. What can I do to deliver them?" And just then He sees a
shadow on the wall outside His office, and He says to Gabriel,
"Whose shadow is that?" Gabriel says, "That's Hosea's shadow."
Who was Hosea? You Bible students know that Hosea was that
Old Testament prophet who, when his wife was unfaithful to
him, came to this conclusion, that, just as he had to suffer to
bring back his wayward wife, so God suffers to bring back His
erring children. And so when God sees Hosea's shadow there, He
says, "Does that mean that even God must suffer?" "Yes," said
Gabriel, "that's what it means." So in the next scene, God's looking down again, and He says, "I see a young man carrying a cross
up a hill."

That's the fourth act of our drama. That's what we're approaching now, this incarnation that leads up at Easter to the
atonement of our Lord. Here's God, the great, high and holy
One. He doesn't wait yonder in lonely grandeur. He comes. He
invades this world. He comes in the form of One who could walk
among us, One who could live and teach with such beautiful
lyric beauty that His parables linger across the centuries. One
who could stop and heal by the wayside, and put new power into
people, One who could take the blush of shame from a Mag-
dalene's brow. Recall that day, when they brought to him a
woman taken in sin, about to be stoned? Jesus, with that infinite
courtesy, didn't even embarrass her. He simply waited till the
crowd's passion had subsided and then said, "Doth no man con-
demn these? Neither do I. Go, and sin no more."

Over in New Jersey some years ago, a young man committed a
very heinous sin, and his father discovered it just before Sunday
dinner. At dinner that day, the father said to his son, "Son, see
me in my study after dinner." The boy went in, and the father
said to him: "My son, I can't condone what you've done, heinous
beyond words, but, I'm your father. I'll suffer this through with
you. I'll go through it with you." God with us. Immanuel. That's

what we're coming to celebrate at Christmas. And isn't that what we need? The scapegoat method won't do it. Mere morality won't do it. Even the strong helping the weak won't do it. We need a God who can come with us.

A lawyer in Wilkes-Barre, in an address to his fellow alumni at a commencement luncheon, said: "My religious faith can be expressed in a boyhood experience. I was taken by my father to New York City. I was little, and to keep from getting lost I clung to his finger, but after a while, in the crowds and the long steps, I grew tired, and my fingers began to slip, and I looked up to him and said, 'Father, you'll have to take hold of my hand now. I can't hold on much longer.'"

Is that not about where we are today? Even holding on, in our own strength we cannot do it. We need the grip of a God on us. That's exactly the kind of God we have, through the One who came at Christmas time.

# 22

## Peace of Mind Is Not Enough

### By CHARLES B. TEMPLETON

THE FACT THAT THESE ARE TROUBLED AND TULMULTUOUS TIMES needs no authentication by this speaker. It is evident in a thousand circumstances. Under the pressures of the day in which we live, we are beginning to realize that we need resources beyond those we have if we are to face the problems that bear upon us.

The tensions of our time have been much commented about. Some of the comment has been serious, some facetious. It has been suggested that future historians will refer to our generation as "the aspirin and barbiturate age." Someone else, noting that there have been a great many multiple births recently, has wondered if the reason may not be that the world has grown so bad even babies are afraid to come into it alone!

You can see this contemporary tension reflected in the increase of mental illness: it is an appalling fact that one out of two hospital beds in America is for a mental patient. Our tension evidences itself also in the excessive indulgence in alcoholic beverages: the excessive use of alcohol growing out of a failure of nerve. The man with no inner resources seeks a temporary escape

*Charles B. Templeton is secretary of the division of evangelism of the Presbyterian Church, U.S.A. He was a former staff evangelist for the National Council of Churches.*

from pressure and responsibility in the illusion of well-being that alcohol induces. Further evidence of tension is to be seen in the suicide rate which is astonishingly high.

The deep disquiet of the century has revealed itself also in more positive ways. More people belong to the churches in America that at any previous time in history. Church membership increases at a pace swifter than the growth of the population. Church attendance has reached an all-time high. It is a rare city that does not have a number of churches forced to conduct two or three (in one case, seven) identical morning services in order to house those who crowd the doors seeking solace and the equipment with which to face the problems of living.

Probably the unique evidence of our contemporary tension is what has been described as the "peace of mind literature." It had its beginning some years ago when an eminent Jewish rabbi, Joshua Loth Liebman, wrote *Peace of Mind*. It was a phenomenal success. It was soon followed by a book by the nationally known Roman Catholic Bishop, Fulton J. Sheen. Then came a literal rash of books, hundreds of titles, all purporting to suggest how, through religio-psychological technique, one might equip oneself to live with peace, poise, power, serenity and so on. This phenomenon reached its zenith in an advertisement appearing in the literary supplement of the Sunday *New York Times* where it was proclaimed in bold, black type, "NOW YOU CAN HAVE PEACE OF MIND IN TEN MINUTES!" All one had to do was to send a publisher $3.98 and he would ship the paper panacea postpaid!

Of course, this kind of thing is sheer, unadulterated balderash! There are no simple answers to life and anyone who offers some simple little mental gymnastic by which the pressures are lessened as a solution to the complex problems of living is a charlatan. It should be made clear, of course, that some of the books referred to above are practical and helpful; many, however, are claptrap, glossing over the real problems and offering but temporary sur-cease.

It is my purpose to speak to you about this matter of "peace of mind." Is there a genuine inner tranquillity that may be known by our harassed generation? There is; a peace of mind that comes to us only from God, through Jesus Christ, His Son. "Peace" is peculiarly a New Testament word. There is a sort of parenthesis of peace around the entire ministry of Jesus. When he was born, the heavens were filled with the song of the angels, "Peace on Earth." When he grew up to begin his ministry among men, his language was constantly studded with the word "peace." When he came to the end of his days and met with a group of his disciples, one of his last words was, "My peace I leave with you."

We are always interested in what a prominent person leaves when he dies. Some rich man dies and the newspaper reports his estate. We are always interested in what he leaves. We often for-get, of course, that he leaves *everything!* I heard of a family having a discussion about the death of a famous man. They were sitting around the kitchen table talking about it. Someone asked, "What did he leave?" Before anyone could answer, Grandma, seated in the corner, said, "Everything!"

What did Jesus have to leave behind him when he came to the end of life? He had nothing in terms of physical possessions. Someone has said that when Jesus left this world all he had to leave behind was four nails and two jagged pieces of wood on which he had been crucified. Even his robe was stripped from him. But he had something more; he had his peace to leave. He said to his disciples even as he says to men today, "My peace I leave with you." When he came from the grave and met the disciples, craven and hiding in an upper room in Jerusalem, his first word to them was the Jewish greeting, "sholom"—peace. Around the entire ministry of Jesus there was a parenthesis of peace.

If any word needs to be spoken to this generation, this is that word. All of life is a war; a war against poverty, against illness, against disillusionment, against worry, against failure, against a thousand antagonists. Anyone who has lived very long gets rid of any brash optimism he may have had about life. Those who know people know that behind the façade men put up to others there are troubles and difficulties. And if any word needs to be spoken, especially in our hectic twentieth century, it is this word, "peace."

And none can bring it save the God who made us. Jesus, "the Prince of Peace," has declared more armistices in the souls of men than anyone in history. If men and women will but come to him and lay down their arms of rebellion and turn from the seeking of their own purposes and begin to be concerned to live their lives in obedience to his will, he can accomplish the inexplicable. He can bring to pass in our turbulent, confused, frustrated and frantic age "a peace which passeth all understanding," a peace that comes only with the knowledge of sins forgiven, the release from guilt and the knowledge that life has begun anew.

I know the word "peace" sounds incongruous today. I'm sure it sounded incongruous in Jesus' day. It may be that someone in this audience may say rather testily, "Why, Mr. Templeton, do you speak of peace? Why do you cry peace in a world where there is no peace? We move from headline to headline, from hot war to cold war. We stand on the edge of an abyss, with the nations of the world glowering over an iron curtain, triggering their earthquakes and preparing, perhaps, the annihilation of life. How can you, when in one generation we have seen three wars, glibly speak of peace?"

The word sounded just as incongruous in Jesus' day. When the angels filled the air with song and shouted, "Peace. Fear not," might not the shepherds have looked up and said, "What do you mean, 'Peace'? There is no peace, except the Pax Romana, a peace of arms. We are ground under the dictator's heel. We live in a world where human life is cheap and where the best music Romans know is the clanking chains of their captives. We live in a world where men are counted as chattels, where ugliness is all about us and where horror is commonplace. What do you mean, 'Peace'?''

Mary, in the stable, might have looked up and said, "What do you mean, 'Fear not'? There is Herod to fear; he is after my Son's life. There is that long journey into Egypt to fear. There are brigands on the road to fear. There is the evil in men's hearts that, even now, casts the shadow of a cross across my Baby's life. What do you mean, 'Fear not'?" It did sound incongruous then, just as it does today.

Now, what is this peace of God? Does the peace of God mean that, somehow, all problems are solved and man goes to heaven on a flowery bed of ease? Does it mean that Christians have no problems and that life is lived "at ease"? Oh no, friend! If you want to see the Author of peace, look at Calvary. There, in the midst of agony, you may catch a glimpse of the kind of peace that God gives.

Look at the picture. We've seen it a thousand times. There, in the midst of the hateful shouting of the mob, are three crosses, stark and silhouetted against the horizon. Everywhere there is noise, tumult, confusion. People passing by on the way to the city wag their heads and jeer as they go. The horses are neighing with the scent of blood in their nostrils. The Roman soldiers are clanging their armor and holding the crowd back with their pikestaffs. Hear the groaning cries of the thieves as they die, the weeping women at the foot of the cross, the noise of the people who jeer and hoot and catcall, "Come down, if you really are the Christ."

But there is one place of peace at the heart of the tumult. It is on the central cross where, in an unutterable welter of agony,

Christ thinks not of himself but of the people who are doing this to him, and cries, "Father, forgive them; for they know not what they do." He thinks not of himself but of the thief in a similar agony, and says to him, "Today you will be with me in paradise." That's the kind of peace God brings. Not separation from the world's pain, not a release from the world's problems, not an apartness from the horror and heartbreak that often lies at the heart of contemporary living, but a peace like that often found at the heart of a storm.

I was in Halifax, Nova Scotia, three summers ago when a hurricane swept across the eastern seaboard. The winds went to 120 miles an hour. I remember peering out the window, watching. Anything elemental moves me deeply. I saw the result of the winds and heard the incredible howling and felt the house shudder as I stood and watched, entranced. Then the heart of the storm passed directly over the city. I had always heard there was a calm at the heart of a storm. I thought the phrase was a piece of literary license. I thought it would be a relative calm, But suddenly the sun came out. There were a few scattered clouds and no breeze at all. You experienced an exhilarating feeling, perhaps because of the lessened pressure. There we stood, in the midst of a magnificent, sunny day, at the heart of a tremendous tumult of storm.

Now hear this; the peace that God brings doesn't set you apart from the tumult, but at the heart of it; in the midst of a world seemingly gone mad, you stand with God, with an inner serenity, with an inner peace, with the certain knowledge that God's will will be done. He brings within the soul a sense of a rightness, the knowledge that life is going somewhere, that you have found the meaning at the heart of the universe. This is the true peace of mind, the "peace which passeth all understanding," that comes only from God, through Jesus Christ our Lord.

But there is also a false peace of mind. There is a vogue in our time, a pseudo-psychological approach to preaching that suggests to men and women they can find the answers to life simply by adjusting to life, by coming to terms with life. There is some truth in it of course but, as with all half-truths, there is danger in it as well. Many people are using this gospel of peace of mind as a sort of patent medicine with which to quiet their nerves and to release their tensions. Christianity is too often turned into little less than a success cult: the end of life becomes success and health and happiness.

I have a friend, a businessman in Toronto. He came one day driving a great black Cadillac. I looked at him and jokingly said, "You're very prosperous these days." He turned and in sudden seriousness said, "Why, God gave me this Cadillac." I said, "That's interesting." He said, "I think God wants His children to have the best." I said, "You know, it's interesting that God gave you a Cadillac; He gave His only begotten son a cross. He gave His first and best disciple decapitation, imprisonment, stoning, shipwreck and all the thousand other troubles that he faced."

We must rid our minds of the idea that Christianity is designed to help us to come to terms with life, to adjust to it, to resolve our problems by "holding good thoughts" or by simply "thinking positively." There are some people today with "peace of mind" who have no right to it; a woman of my acquaintance, for instance, who has left three marriages in wreckage behind her. Of the three marriages there have been three children. All of the children are in boarding schools while she goes traipsing around the country, following popular preachers and professing to have found "peace of mind." Well, if she has found it, she has no right to it! Look at the wreckage of those three marriages and at those three children deprived of a home and of a mother's love and a father's care. She should be profoundly disquieted, not at peace.

It is no boon to tell a man he can find peace of mind until he has faced up to the fundamental ill at the heart of life; his alienation from God. You don't prescribe aspirin for cancer. You don't give some palliative for a tumor of the brain. No life can be what it ought to be until that life is right in its relationship to God, until we have asked and found His forgiveness for our pride and self-will and, in the knowledge of His love, have begun to live our lives as He would have them lived.

The trouble with much ministry in our time is that it has fallen into a sort of subservience to psychiatry. Many a minister hardly dares to say anything about human behavior unless he looks for approval to a psychiatrist. Psychiatry, a young science, has made many notable contributions to our thinking. We owe an everlasting debt to these men who have plumbed the nether regions of the mind and have told us things about human behavior that we never knew before. But we need to remember this: psychiatry cannot meet the deepest needs of the soul. Psychiatry is fundamentally negative.

I have a friend in Topeka, Kansas, a psychoanalyst at the Menninger Clinic, one of the outstanding psychiatric clinics in America. Discussing his work he said to me, "I am two people in my work. As a psychiatrist I'm interested in getting my patients 'symptom free.' What they do after that is none of my business as a psychiatrist except that they observe the laws of mental health. But," he said, "as a Christian, this is where I begin." One of the great psychiatrists of our day has said, "Psychiatry can untangle the twisted skein of a man's affairs, but it offers no new pattern for the reweaving." Psychiatry and Christianity complement each other. Where the first leaves off the second begins.

We need to remember this; we are not to come to terms with this world, we are to change it! We are not to adjust to it for it is out of joint. It is upside down and needs to be turned right side up. There is a false peace of mind which is only a temporary alleviation of the real problem of the alienation of our life from God.

Now let me come to the thing I want to impress upon you especially; that peace of mind is not a legitimate Christian goal. Jesus knew nothing of what is commonly called "peace of mind." Indeed, Jesus was, you might put it, maladjusted to the status quo. He was so disturbed at times he could not sleep at night, but prayed through till the morning. Jesus seldom lived in peace; he lived in the center of turmoil. Everywhere he went there were riots and uprisings and difficulties. Jesus knew that the world was wrong and, striving to bring it to the will of the Father, he stirred up many animosities. Someone has said, "They didn't crucify Christ because he said, 'Behold the lilies of the field how they grow,' They crucified him because he insisted on saying, 'Behold the thieves in the temple, how they steal.' " And that's a very different kind of doctrine!

The same was true of the early Church; they were disturbers who turned their world upside down. The ideal Christian experience is not peace of mind, it is a sort of "discontented contentment"—a contentment in that you have found the meaning at the heart of life, you have found God; but at the same time a divine discontent in your soul that will not let you settle down in somnolence and ease to live as you will. You are under a divine compulsion. You must go out and try to set your world aright. Indeed, how can any Christian want to settle down in some selfish kind of serenity in a world so full of injustice, so full of inequity, so full of war, so full of poverty and hate and ugliness and evil? How can any Christian want to settle down and live in some kind of insular comfort and fail to come to grips with life, to fight injustice, to fight darkness and paganism and evil and ugliness no matter what its guise? We must struggle in the name of Christ and do it redemptively and compassionately that men and women may be won and may come to know him as Saviour and to live for him as Lord.

This is not only the message of the Church. Interestingly enough psychiatry at its best says the same thing. Jung, in his book *Modern Man in Search of a Soul,* said this, "I have never been able to effect a lasting cure in any of my patients until the patient has discovered a living and creative faith in God."

That is what psychiatry says. This is what Jesus says; he stood before a crowd and saw them "as sheep without a shepherd." Seeing these poor bewildered people, he lifted his arms and cried out to them, "Come unto me, all ye that labor. . . ." All ye that are frustrated and confused and mixed up and troubled, and burdened . . . "come unto me and I will give you rest." I will give you a deep-down peace within and a "divine discontent" as you go out to touch the world and to win it to my will.

# 23

## Christianity in a Revolutionary World

### By ELTON TRUEBLOOD

NOT LONG AGO IN THE CITY OF LONDON I WAS WALKING DOWN
to Kings Cross station to buy a ticket to go to Scotland the next
day and as I walked almost opposite the great St. Pancras
Church, I heard a sound. It was a loud sound coming from an
area near the sidewalk, so I followed it. There in an area perhaps
200 feet long and 150 feet wide, I saw a crowd of people standing. Into the center was a man on a box. I went closer to see who
the man was, and, as I got close enough, I could easily tell, because the words on the box were "The St. Pancras Communist
Party." The man was speaking extraordinarily well, with
abundant confidence. By him was a portable loud speaker on
wheels, which he was ready to take to another place and set up
again in order to proceed with his persuasive efforts.

As I looked all around the crowd to see what kind of people
they were and what was going on, I noticed that there were
young girls, fourteen or fifteen years of age, circulating in the
crowd selling literature, especially *The Daily Worker*. All of
them were intent upon their job. I listened for a while and then

*Elton Trueblood is on leave as professor of philosophy at Earl-
ham College to serve as chief of religious information for the
U. S. Information Agency, Washington, D. C.*

went on down to Kings Cross, and a half hour later, when I had bought the ticket, I came back. Again I heard the sound. Again I went in and this time I saw that the speaker was another man, the first having, no doubt, finished what he had to say. More people had come in and the affair was going on with vigor. Other young girls were again in the crowd distributing literature and I knew that I was observing something of remarkable power.

Then I looked across the street at the outline of St. Pancras Church, one of the great churches of London, built soon after the battle of Waterloo. All was dark, without a sound. The apparent power was in a movement in which the men were saying things which I hated, things which disturbed me terribly, things which seemed to be unfair, but, oh how persuasive they sounded to many of the people. As I walked back to the hotel I knew that I had seen an important sight, and one that reveals something about our world.

Now why were the people so glad to go off the street to listen to these men? You wonder, don't you? Don't you often say, "Why would so many people be carried away by what seems to us so obviously a false doctrine? How could it be that so many millions in China, including many of those who were formerly in the Church, are now strong and powerful members of the Communist party and have given up Christianity?"

Recently the chancellor of Yenching University in Peking was forced to go on trial and was found guilty of being opposed to the regime. Who do you suppose was the chief witness against him? It was his eighteen year old daughter, who maintained that her father was a reactionary. She felt that she represented the new teeming, surging, youthful life of tomorrow to which her father, the distinguished president of the University, was opposed. She testified that he had sown the seeds of doubt in her mind.

All this seems very surprising. We say, "How could it be?" The reason for it is very complex, but one aspect is this: *We are today in one of the great revolutionary periods of the world.* It is not the first and it will not be the last. We know something of the revolution that came at the end of the eighteenth century, of which the American Revolution was one phase and the French Revolution another. We know that this had some ugly aspects, especially in France. We all know something of the Revolution of 1848, especially in Germany, which sent so many fine people to this country, including Carl Schurz.

Now, it seems we are in a third period of revolution which has marked these last two centuries. It is worldwide and it takes many forms. We know something of the form that it has taken in India. Here were hundreds of millions of people, who had been under alien rule, without full liberties and without full equality, but especially without social equality. And now in our own time India and Pakistan have both become independent nations, because of a great upsurge of revolutionary zeal.

We know something of what is going on in South Africa. Night after night come reports of many people being sent to jail. It is a terrible time, but it is a time when men who have not been given equality or opportunity or the same privileges as other men are finding ways of demanding those privileges. It has some dangers, but, with its fundamental drive, we, as Christians, are bound to have sympathy.

Or take West Africa. There are a good many students in this country from West Africa, especially Nigeria and the Gold Coast, and some of these are among the most brilliant, able and forward-looking students that we have in our American colleges and universities. Do you know what these young men say? They say they are going home to be the Washingtons and the Jeffersons of their country. It is possible that Nigeria, in a short time, may get dominion status and be just as much an independent country as Canada or Australia and all this is occurring under the leadership of the native people, who are showing remarkable ability. They demand that they be given the same opportunities that other people have sought for themselves and their children.

Something of what is going on in Persia is bound to be understood in the same way, even though the revolution has been harmful to many. The driving out of the British technicians brought the Persian oil industry to a standstill. If you talk with some of the young Persians who are studying in this country, they will tell you that, though they have oil in such tremendous quantities, very little of the economic gain has heretofore reached the poor people of Iran. They are absolutely adamant that, in some way or other, they shall get some of the advantage of it, so that their education can be lifted and their poverty overcome and so that they have opportunities similar to those which we have in this country.

In every case there is a drive for emancipation, for freedom, for equality, but in every case there are also ugly aspects that go along with that drive.

In China, apparently, we see the extreme case, in the modern world, of this double truth. The drive is extreme; the ugliness is extreme. We are helped in the effort to understand something of the reason for this situation when we learn how large the average farm has been in China. It is less than one acre. The beautiful countryside of Indiana and Illinois is dotted with magnificent farms where frequently one farmer will have twenty-five thousand dollars' worth of machinery, where many of the men farm four or five hundred acres, where farmers have large bank accounts and where they have all the great opportunities of the city plus the opportunities of their farm life. When you ride across the countryside and look at them, try to think what it must be like in a country where the average farm is *less than one acre.* How would you like to support your family on that much land? Most of us have never tried anything like it.

It came to me very vividly one winter in Texas. I was invited out to spend the night with some friends of mine, on what was described locally as a small ranch, since it included only two thousand acres. As I lay in bed in the ranch house, I could hear the lowing of the cattle over the beautiful Texas hills. Here were two thousand acres to support one family, and then I thought of the other people of the world, for whom this situation would seem so fantastic that they couldn't even believe that it exists anywhere in the world. As I lay there, and couldn't sleep, I knew better than I had known before something of why ours is a revolutionary world. Specifically I understood why the idea of land reform has a potent appeal to the submerged peoples of the world.

Now what is to be the Christian attitude toward all of this? The forces of the Christian faith have a terrible temptation to-day, and the temptation is this: *We see the evils that go along with these revolutionary movements, the killing, the hatred, the bitter struggle, the recriminations, and we tend to turn our backs upon the entire business.* We tend to say, "This is evil, let us have nothing to do with it." But this is an awful temptation for the simple reason that such a reaction puts the forces of Christianity wholly on the side of the conservatives, the rich, the favored nations, the old people who appear to the other people of the world to be trying to hold on to what they have out of self-indulgence and a love of power. If we allow ourselves to be maneuvered into such a position, we shall lose almost every bit of our influence in this world. In that case the Church may go on, but it will go on as a small side issue, away from the main center, and something new will have to come to unite with this revolutionary power, *for ours is a revolutionary age whether we like it or not.* We shall not stop it! *The thing for us to do is to*

*know this and to find our right place in it. It will go on and it*
*will increase, because ours is a century of storm.*

In all its great periods, the Christian faith has been a revolutionary faith. Look again at the 17th Chapter of Acts. What it
says is that the early Christians in the Roman Empire were
looked upon as revolutionaries and subversives, who were turning the world against Caesar to another king, namely, Christ.
Consequently, it was said of them, "These are the men who
have turned the world upside down." That is what the Christian
revolution means. We should have known this all along if we
had listened carefully to the words of the mother of Jesus.

He hath shewed strength with his arm; he hath scattered the
proud in the imagination of their hearts. He hath put down the
mighty from their seats, and exalted them of low degree. He hath
filled the hungry with good things; and the rich he hath sent empty
away.

The *Magnificat* is a revolutionary document! In its great
periods Christianity, instead of simply glossing over the present
order, the pagan order, the worldly order, has always challenged
the secular order at point after point. See what happened in the
emancipation of women. The Christian faith very early began to
give women the same status in most areas as men. Even in the
New Testament we find the great sentence, "In Christ there is
neither bond nor free, neither male nor female." Christianity
was bound, in time, to overcome both slavery and discrimination
on the basis of sex. It was through the Christian faith that the
first real change came in the treatment of prisoners in jails and
penitentiaries. And so the figure of the beautiful Elizabeth Fry,
going into Newgate Prison, is one of the glorious figures in the
history of the Christian faith.

Christians were the first who tried to overcome slavery in this
country and in the British colonies and we know the names of

the people who did it for conscience' sake. Very largely the labor movement in both Britain and America came through Christian auspices in the first instance. I have heard it said in Britain that John Wesley had more to do with the coming of the labor movement in Britain than Karl Marx. This was because John Wesley, by his evangelical revival, took common men at the head of mine pits and gave a new dignity to their lives as the followers of Jesus Christ and, therefore, equal to all of their brothers under the Fatherhood of God.

Christianity, when it is vital, shakes men, changes them. It changes the order by which they live. *Never forget, therefore, that Christianity is a revolutionary faith.* What then is our right relation to the revolutionary movements of our age? Certainly not just to stand off and have nothing to do with them. That is to make ourselves irrelevant. Certainly we ought not to try to oppose them, for that is to try to do the impossible. *The way of wisdom, remembering the genius of the Christian faith, is to acknowledge the revolutionary movement, to glory in it, to be glad that people want their freedom and their equality and the dignity of their lives, but, at the same time, to seek to guide the revolutionary movement aright so that it will not go into the dangerous and cruel aspects which a revolutionary movement will enter unless it is guided by something like the Gospel.* The revolutionary movements, without the Gospel, are almost sure to be cruel and ultimately totalitarian, as was demonstrated in the Reign of Terror in France long ago. Let us bring these revolutionary desires of men into the orbit of the Christian faith. Instead of trying to oppose the revolutionary desires of our time, let us head the procession, take the people who are trying to get justice and help them to get justice in a Christian way. This will surely be one of the major ways in which a better world can be born.

It is an awful thing to hear some of the people from Europe

talk about the Christian faith. Many are almost afraid to use the Christian terms and when asked the reason for their hesitation they say, "Oh, the Christian religion is allied with the corrupt politics of the old parties. It's the old regime, and we are looking for something new." That hurts when you hear it, but we can understand because in many cases that has been the exact situation.

Dear friends, in so far as we have anything to do with it, let us determine that such will never be the situation here. We have a chance to keep the Christian movement bold, fluid, progressive, new, not simply trying to hold things as they are, but attacking evil wherever it appears, including ourselves, and bringing to bear the mighty dynamic of the Christian faith to overcome it. The notion that every man is created equal in the sight of the living God is the most revolutionary single idea in the world. And it will finally, if understood and followed, break through every barrier, every prejudice, every wall of hatred. We must make the Christian faith far more bold. It must be made more demanding. If the salt loses its savor, it is worth nothing. It is only if it keeps its saltiness, its vigor and its tang that it is able to affect the kind of world in which we live.

# 24

## Turning the Corner

### By LESLIE D. WEATHERHEAD

I'D LIKE TO TALK TO YOU, IF I MAY, FROM THE TEXT IN PSALM 59:10, which in our version sounds very interesting: "The God of my mercy shall prevent me."

We remember that the word "prevent" means "to go before." I want to suggest a better translation, quite accurate: "My God, in His loving-kindness, shall meet me at every corner." I don't know whether you know over here the name of Mr. Hugh Redwood. He has written many books. He is a journalist, just retiring after a magnificent career in Fleet Street, which is the heart of our newspaper world in London. And on one occasion he was tired and going through a time of great strain, and had a big meeting before him, and his hostess with whom he was staying said, "Would you like to escape the chatter of these people down here and slip up for half an hour's quiet?" And he went up to a room where there was a fire burning, and an armchair drawn up to it, and on the table near his elbow was an open Bible, and this verse was underscored, and somebody had written in the margin the translation I have just given you: "My God, in His loving-kindness, shall meet me at every corner."

*Leslie D. Weatherhead is the pastor of City Temple (Congregational), London.*

237

That is the message I would like to bring to you. I would like first of all, quite quickly to run through those "corners" which meet us all from the cradle to the grave, and see how relevant this passage is for all of them. For instance, our psychologists talk about the "menaces" of life. We must put the word "menace" in inverted commas, because they use the word "menace" in regard to marriage—which you'll agree it need not always be, but sometimes is! And they mean by the use of the word that just around the corner, again and again in life, there is something which we must meet with courage and serenity. The mastery of the art of living depends on whether we can meet these successive demands without fear, without running away from them. They begin very early. They go on until death.

Now let us imagine first of all a family in which there are three little children. The first goes to school, the second goes to school, the third knows that there is coming very quickly a time when he won't be able to choose whether to play in the garden or play in the nursery. He *must* go to school. The menace of that demand is just around the corner. Would you believe me if I say that in the psychological clinic in which I work in London with seven Christian medically trained psychiatrists, again and again we find that there are people of mature life who always take the attitude of fear and anxiety about anything that is strange and unknown, because they formed that habit, that "pattern of reaction" as we call it, in those very early days. Nobody helped them when there came the terrifying demand of leaving home and its security, and going to school, and now, although they are grown up, anything sudden or strange or demanding finds them afraid and scared. Now it isn't too early to tell them the message tonight that there is a Friend for little children, not up "above the bright blue sky," but very close, and very wise, and very strong, who will help them at that corner.

Then there is the corner which we have to meet when we

decide what we are going to do with our lives. Perhaps more important for the boy, yet not always so, for all girls do not marry. I feel there that we should give our children absolute freedom as far as what they want to do is reasonable. I would implore parents present not to decide in five minutes what a human being should do for fifty years. So often Father says, "Oh, he can go into my office," or Mother says, "Oh, she can take up typing," and sometimes a man wants the family business to be carried on in the same name. My friends, it is much more important that a human being should be happy, than that the immortal name "Tompkins" should go on forever. Let us, if we can, say to our children: "God will meet you in this situation. God really does guide you. If you trust Him He doesn't let you make a mistake." Because the happy people in the world are the people who love doing what they have to do. The unhappy people, the imprisoned, fettered, inhibited people, are so often people who have been very quickly thrust into a job for which they have no wish at all, and no capabilities, and yet they are tied down to their job, and they only begin to live when the clock says they can stop work. Let us claim freedom for them, and tell them of the God who will meet them at every corner.

Then I think of the corner we call sex consciousness and marriage. Here is the dream of a girl of seventeen. I can only give you my word that this is an authentic dream, and not made up to illustrate the sermon, although it sounds like it. It is taken from a book by Maurice Nicoll, called *Dream Psychology*. One might say in brackets that if you keep on dreaming the same dream over and over again, you can be sure it is a message to you, either from the depths of your own mind or from high heaven—and perhaps they are the same thing. Perhaps your mind, at its deepest level, is in very close touch with the Eternal Creative Mind. I believe it is. This girl kept on dreaming this: "I am safely in my home when there comes a knock on my door. I open the door and there is a strange soldier. He grabs me, he takes me down the street of which I have familiar knowledge, and then he turns a corner into a street that is confusing and bewildering—and I wake up crying." You see what is happening. She is beginning already to know that very likely someone will come and take her from the security of the home into a strange life that is confusing and demanding, and she doesn't know what the demands that are going to be made upon her are going to be like. What a chance for the good mother to talk about the God for whom sex is a perfectly natural, an utterly beautiful thing, that shouldn't be spoiled but kept holy! What a chance for that mother to talk of the God who will meet her daughter at every corner!

And I think we should say a word about the women who do not marry. I always think it is very cheap and very poor fun to make jokes about them—such jokes are much more cruel than they are funny. In my church in London, whenever I find some fine work being done unselfishly in some situation, I find un-married women of middle age doing it. One wants to say to them, that although their lot is difficult because they have love to give and they can't fully express it, Jesus wasn't married. And though they feel frustration, there is God there, waiting to lead them round that corner.

One such woman in the clinic to which I have referred said to a psychologist friend of mine who was helping her, "You know, you made one day last week the happiest day of my life." He said, "Why was that?" She said, "Because you gave me courage no longer to try to look twenty years younger than I am." Wasn't that fine of her! Wasn't it splendid of her to be so honest! Because one might underline this sentence: that the first law of mental health and inner peace is to be utterly honest with yourself. Let us give the benefit of any doubt there may be to another. Let us be ruthlessly honest about ourselves. Do you know this prayer? It was written by an American, Reinhold Niebuhr, one of your great scholars and theologians: "O God, help me to change those things which can and should be changed. [Give me courage to do that.] O God, help me to accept those things that cannot be changed. [O God, give me patience to do that.] And O God, help me to know the difference. [And give me insight to know that.]" It is so important to accept, to go forward to the next corner with acceptance and joy, remembering our text.

And why shouldn't we say a word to those who are aging? How often a business is driven into the ditch because an old man will not relinquish the wheel to a younger man, and will almost wreck the business because he doesn't want to give up power! How often a woman will make her home miserable because she tries to bring up her daughter-in-law's children for her, and tell her how the home should be run! And yet how beneficent and lovely, ripe with wisdom and understanding, ready for the advice when it is asked, how lovely a thing, like the tints of your Fall in the woods, how lovely a thing can old age be!

And am I talking to somebody who is afraid of dying? That is around the corner. It may be around the corner at any moment. I would like to bring the message of our text to such. I would like, for instance, to tell them that I have been myself nearly forty years in the Christian ministry, including service in the army in the First World War and chaplaincy duty in Persia and Mesopotamia and India—I have never seen anybody die unhappy. Death is sometimes sudden. Death is sometimes, indeed most often, unconscious, but if people are conscious right up to the last minute, my evidence—and I've never seen it refuted by any doctor or any nurse or any minister—my evidence is that one of the most wonderful experiences in the world is to die. I sat on a man's bed not long ago, holding his hand. I must have held his hand tightly, because he pulled it away and said, "Don't hold me back! I want to go on! It looks wonderful farther on!"

My own sister, thought to be dying, heard the doctor say to

the nurse, "She won't get through tonight." She said afterward that that news was good news to her, because already she felt as though she were glimpsing something very wonderful. When she knew that she was going to recover she heard the news with dismay. It was so hard to come back. Lazarus, they say, was a disappointed, melancholy man until the end, because he had seen too much. One of our greatest surgeons, William Hunter, on his deathbed said, "If I only had strength to lift a pen, I would write, 'How wonderful and pleasant a thing it is to die.' " And after all, isn't that just like God to meet us at that corner? If you had had the consciousness, you would have been afraid of being born. You wouldn't have wanted to emerge from that secure, cozy, warm life where you had lived for nine months, and yet there were arms that received you, and eyes that smiled into yours, and people who wanted you and held you fast. Will He who brought us through that, desert us at death? Is He not the God who in His loving-kindness will meet me at that last corner of all?

Men and women, why is it that we have so misunderstood Christianity that we think it is a kind of insurance against calamity—that we shall be delivered from those things which other people have to face? Who ever taught you that by saying your prayers you could escape falling bombs, financial disaster, cancer of the body, hurt of the mind, disease? It is not in the New Testament. Jesus never said that. Some Psalmist may have said it because he hadn't seen the vision which Jesus gave to the world. Jesus never said to his men, "Men, if you follow Me, you'll escape the corners that other men have to turn. You'll be let off the things that other people face." He said they would be persecuted *because* they were his. Men and women, if you asked that from God, I want to explain to you, you are asking Him to be *less* loving, not more loving.

The world is a school. How do we expect ever to get through

school without examinations that try us and test us and make us able to face the next stage of our career? This life on earth is the lowest form in God's school. Is it a good father who lets us off school? I can remember my own school days. I dreaded them, I hated them, I feared them. And I sat next a boy—I can see him now, a great fat fellow without a care in the world. I can remember his nickname. It was Fatty West. Wouldn't it be fun if he was sitting in this audience! He had the most wonderful father that a boy ever had, because if the sun shone, Mr. West didn't mind if Fatty turned out to school or if he didn't, and if there were examinations my friend could escape them and play, but my horrible, cruel, heartless, unkind father expected me to go to school whether it was fine or wet, whether there were examinations or no examinations, but now I know which was the finer father, and now I know who showed the greater love. How do we expect to get away without the tests of school?

Jesus never said, "I will deliver you from the waters." Jesus said, "When you pass through the waters, I shall be with you." He carried that message from the Old Testament, and drove it home, and isn't that the golden cord that runs through the whole Bible? Enoch walked with God. Abraham was the friend of God. The message came to Moses: "Certainly I will be with thee." And so on through the prophets and the poets. Micah: "What doth the Lord require of thee, but to do justly, and to love mercy, and to walk humbly with thy God?" David has said he's not going to fear the valley of the shadow, because God is with him. That's the clue. "I will be *with you*. With you. With you. With you."

Jesus is no ascetic, retreating to the mountains. He is with his men. He loves his men. He loves every phase of man's life. He got into trouble for going to parties. And when he passes from earthly sight he says, "Lo, I am with you every day unto the end of the world." If you are going to remember one sentence from this sermon, could it be this: that because he is with us in all our difficulties, he transmutes our troubles into our training. My God in His loving-kindness will meet you tomorrow morning. He will be with you all through the day, far more eager to find you than you are to find Him.

I must push the message home with one true story taken from the First World War, where a man who was a close friend with another—they were like David and Jonathan—watched his friend go from our British trenches into what we called in those terrible days "No Man's Land," the ground between the enemy trenches and our own. He saw his friend hit with a bullet, saw his friend fall, and he said to his officer, "Sir, he's my friend. We've been very close. Can I go out and bring him in?" And the officer said, "No, of course you can't. Look at the fire that is going on out there. Nobody could live out there. Your friend is mortally wounded and if you go you'll be mortally wounded too, and I'll lose both of you." But before the officer had finished speaking the man was off, and the officer watched. Somehow that hero got his friend onto his shoulder and he staggered with him back into the home trenches, but his friend was dead, and he himself was mortally wounded, and the officer was very angry and upset, and he said, "I told you! I told you it wasn't worth it. He's dead and now you're mortally wounded, just as I said." The hero looked up into the officer's face with his dying eyes and he said this, "It was worth it, sir." "Worth it?" asked the officer, "How could it be worth it?" "It was worth it because when I got to him he said, 'Jim, I knew you'd come. I knew you'd come.' "

Yes. He doesn't say that his way, the way of Christ, which I think is the clue to the meaning of all living, means that you escape anything that other people have to face. You have to turn every corner, as other people do. But he says, "I will be with you." "Yea, though I walk through the valley of the shadow of death, I will fear no evil, for Thou are *with me*."

# 25

## Freedom's Holy Light

### By *LUTHER W. YOUNGDAHL*

IN THE LAST WAR HAZEL PARKER GAVE US A BEAUTIFUL PHILOSO-
phy of freedom as she said: "Freedom is like a man standing at
night opening the gate latch and sitting for a while on the porch
smoking his pipe before he goes to bed. It is a righteous anger of
pulpits. It is the violence of an argument outside of an election
poll. It is the warm laughter of a girl on the park bench. It is the
unafraid faces of people looking out the windows of a train as it
speeds across the continent. It is the shoulders of a mountain supporting the sky, the seas breaking over the wide sands somewhere,
the air you breathe and the dirt that is in your garden. It is
Lindbergh's appeasing voice raised above a thousand hisses. It
is Westbrook Pegler telling the Roosevelts how to raise their
children. It is the Roosevelts letting them raise themselves. It is
you trying to remember the words of 'The Star Spangled Banner.'
It is the lack of apprehension of the sound of approaching foot-
steps outside your door. It is all the things you feel and cannot
help feeling."

Freedom—it is you—it is I—and just as freedom is you and

*Luther W. Youngdahl is a federal judge in the U. S. District
Court for the District of Columbia.*

245

it is I, just so do you and I determine whether we are going to continue to enjoy it.

Events are constantly occurring around the world which are a grim reminder that we cannot take our freedom for granted. The struggle for freedom never ends. Freedom is not a self-perpetuating privilege. It needs constant nourishment and attention. Because we had freedom yesterday and we enjoy it today, doesn't mean that we are going to continue to enjoy it in the future. People all over the world, almost overnight, have lost the rights and ideals that have taken hundreds of years to win.

We are participants today in an unparalleled struggle for the minds and souls of men. Arrayed on one side are the spiritually barren ideologies which endeavor to uproot the spiritual foundations of our society. On the other side are the cherished spiritual concepts and religious values without which our society would soon pass into oblivion. The forces of freedom and slavery are arraigned against each other in a death struggle, a conflict of arms and propaganda. Lenin realized that if communism was to become world-wide, it would have to be a crusading faith. Democracy will survive only if it becomes a personal possession whose worth and practice are a part of our lives.

At the apex of the power of Rome, when the eagles of her legions had been carried victoriously over all the then known world, the proudest declaration and safeguard and a passport everywhere was *Civis Romanus Sum* (" I am a Roman citizen"). Because the citizens of Rome worshiped at the shrine of bigness and things rather than at the shrine of the spirit, Rome deteriorated and passed into oblivion. This declaration has been succeeded by another, "I am a citizen of the United States."

In this hour of history there is no prouder title than "Citizen of the United States." This declaration is powerful today because in this country there is stressed the philosophy that every individual is created in the image of God and has dignity and because of the reverence accorded to every human life. It is not powerful because of dominion enforced over weaker peoples, for this we have not done; nor because of the fear of territorial expansion at our neighbor's expense, for we have no such ambition; but it is pride-worthy because it means citizenship in a country which is powerful but not predatory, invincible in conflict yet hating war, and a country to which all people may call for relief when under stress of calamity, whether caused by forces of nature or unnatural human forces. We pray that such people may not call in vain.

America is a place, too, where you have the privilege to cast your vote as your conscience dictates, uncoerced by dictator influences—where leaders do not impose their will on you, where your homes cannot be searched without a warrant, where your property is not subject to confiscation, where your family is not put in peril of bodily harm because of your convictions, where you are afforded the opportunity for a richer, fuller life under a government which is subject to, not master of, its citizens.

Last summer I had the opportunity to see thousands of Germans stand in the food lines at the town hall in Berlin. They had come from behind the Iron Curtain to become the recipients of the humanitarian spirit of the people of the United States of America. I feel sure that they would tell us this if they could: "Don't take your freedom for granted, you may lose it."

In the tower of that town hall hangs the great Freedom Bell. I was privileged to be present on United Nations Day, October 24, 1950, with the Crusade for Freedom group when the bell was dedicated and was rung for the first time. Three years later as I heard it ring again in the City Hall tower of Berlin, its message seemed more significant than ever. At twelve noon each day the resonant tones of that illustrious bell are broadcast into Iron Curtain territory, reminding people under the iron heel of the dictator that someday—pray God, soon—they will be free once again. It was paradoxical that in the same town hall where the message of freedom was being rung to the world in such a dramatic way, thousands of hungry people were waiting for their little package of food.

Inscribed on the bell are the words paraphrased from Lincoln's Gettysburg address: "That this world, under God, shall have a new birth of freedom." It is highly important to understand that this inscription stresses the fact that a new birth of freedom must be *under God*. Our freedom comes from God and it will only be under God that we will continue to be free. Our freedom is in peril today because so often we have forgotten God.

Our free way of life was developed by men and women of deep religious faith. Without a continuation of the basic principles on which our nation was founded, the superstructure of our government cannot endure. We have respect for the Founding Fathers, not only because of their historic contributions, but also because they expressed a wisdom and understanding we need today. We cannot assume that our religious heritage will endure. Indeed, it can continue only as we work out for ourselves anew in each generation a sense of urgency and need which inspired them. Religious life requires nourishment and constant care.

The freedom that the colonists sought was the right to seek grace through a personal relationship with God, free from the intervention of other men, the right to human dignity based on this relationship rather than on man-made standards and the moral responsibility and brotherhood arising from this relationship. It was to gain these rights for themselves and for the generations to follow that they staked their lives and their fortunes and forged the American political, economic and social system as set forth in the Declaration of Independence, the Constitution of the United States and the Bill of Rights.

The necessity of religion has been asserted time and again by our great leaders and has found expression in our historic documents. George Washington warned us that "reason and experience both forbid us to expect that national morality can prevail in exclusion of religious principles." From his deathbed in a final warning, he said, "Beware of the man who attempts to inculcate morality without religion."

Thomas Jefferson, whose words are incised on one of the panels of his memorial at the nation's capital, stated that "God who gave us life gave us liberty." "These liberties," Jefferson said, "are the gift of God." If we do not appreciate them and nourish them, we may lose them.

The Founding Fathers declared in the Northwest Ordinance, "Religion, morality and knowledge are necessary to good government and the happiness of mankind." Congress, in designating as our national anthem "The Star Spangled Banner," emphasized the importance of religion. This great anthem calls ours "the heav'n rescued land," praises "the Pow'r that hath made and preserved us a Nation," and avers that "this be our motto, 'In God is our Trust.' "

In the Constitutional Convention, Benjamin Franklin stressed the necessity of prayer and emphasized that if this nation did not place its trust in God, it could not endure. When Franklin came out of the Convention, it is related that a lady asked him, "What shall it be, Mr. Franklin, a monarchy or a republic?" Franklin responded, "A republic, if you can *keep* it." To keep our republic we must keep our religious faith strong.

Then at a later perilous time in our nation's history another great leader called upon the people to place their trust in God. Abraham Lincoln, the Great Emancipator, in the dark days of the Civil War in 1863 just before Thanksgiving Day, urged the people to get down on their knees in penitence, asking forgiveness as he said:

We have been the recipients of the choicest bounties of heaven. We have been preserved these many years in peace and prosperity.

We have grown in numbers, wealth and power as no other nation has ever grown, but we have forgotten God. We have forgotten the gracious Hand which preserved us in peace and multitude and enriched and strengthened us, and we have vainly claimed in the deceitfulness of our hearts that all these blessings were produced by some superior wisdom and virtue of our own. Intoxicated with unbroken success, we have become too self-sufficient to feel the necessity of religion and preserving grace, too proud to pray to the God that made us. It behooves us then to humble ourselves before the offended Power, to confess our national sins, and to pray for forgiveness.

Many have merely a hazy remembrance of the tenets of the American system—the Bill of Rights and some phrases from the Constitution or the Declaration of Independence—but forget the fundamental truths upon which the tenets are based. These truths are the law and the will of God. Only if these are understood and espoused can evil be defeated.

The Western world must do more than build up armaments and stockpile raw materials. As necessary as is military defense in this period of history, we delude ourselves if we think our staggering military budget will save us. We must act with every spiritual resource at our command if we are to win this struggle. Millions of people who are now indifferent to God are unconsciously giving aid, comfort and help to the Communists. A moral breakdown is fast undermining America. We are being seriously threatened from a collapse from inner decay.

Headlines tell only a part of the story of increase in murders and crimes of violence, juvenile delinquency, sex promiscuity, narcotics, graft, corruption and apathy on the part of many. Despite encouragement from increased church attendance in recent years, approximately 50 per cent of our people still remain unchurched. Although United States Sunday School enrollment is at an all-time high (well above the thirty-two million mark), yet twenty-seven million other American children and youth receive little or no church training. Of the one million children who, each year, get into trouble with the law, the vast majority have no record of regular religious instruction.

As in the public schools, Sunday church schools, in many cases, are overcrowded and handicapped by a lack of teachers. As a Christian nation, we cannot afford to let a single child go without his spiritual heritage. Although our stewardship programs and parish work activities have been stepped up in many of our churches, we are still lagging far behind in the amount we appropriate for such work. We spend a far larger sum for horserace betting and for liquor today than we spend for our church schools and humanitarian causes.

Our religion and democracy are so strong that they can never be conquered by open attack. They can only succumb to indifference and neglect. Arnold Toynbee said:

All civilizations which have been destroyed, have destroyed themselves and that even where a civilization's downfall has apparently come from outside forces, external pressures merely reveal the internal weaknesses which antedated the crisis. The fall of the Roman Empire was due largely to internal corruption and in more modern history we note the corruption and lack of respect for law in the French nation was even more dangerous to the French than the German troops on the other side of the Maginot Line.

Ask an American why this country occupies a position as a great world power and he will invariably point to the vast natural resources we possess—the wealth of oil and iron ore, the expanse of forests, the abundance of fertile soil. Or he is likely to point with pride to the productive genius of our people, their ability to invent, their skill as builders of factories, skyscrapers, roads, refrigerators, autos and aircraft. He will undoubtedly boast of our high standard of living and of our proficiency in turning out superior ships, tanks, guns and planes to fight modern war.

But he who has studied the rise and fall of great civilizations of the past knows that such reasons cannot be the answer to a nation's greatness. Important as material resources and technological skills are, they are not the reason for the greatness of a nation.

Character always has been and always will be the keystone of greatness in a person and in a nation. The historian can quickly show us that just as soon as the character of a people begins to weaken and break down, a nation begins to crumble and is on the road downward to ruin. Irreverence, cynicism toward spiritual values, the mad rush for cash, comfort and pleasure—all these are warning signs of dangerous moral deterioration that can destroy us. We need to be most afraid of the danger from within—the corrupting and weakening of national character. It is even more dangerous than the threat of communism from without.

Dynamic Christianity and a militant discipleship are the needs of the hour. A mild form of Christianity makes us immune to the real thing. The call is for a fiery, zealous devotion to Christianity. Never has there been a time when the ardor of discipleship was more needed. We can build a better world, not by parade or panacea, but only by individual consecration.

Fortunately for America and for the world, there seems to be developing a spiritual renaissance. The big event of our age is a spiritual revival that has been growing in the hearts of men. Even secular organizations recognize the necessity of religion. On every side one hears, "America's problem is a spiritual one." Despite our material resources, Americans are searching for confidence, conviction and hope.

Recently it was my privilege to preside at a Prayer Breakfast in our nation's capital and introduce the Chief Justice of the United States to a group of people who are dedicating themselves to the importance of religion in their lives. Prominent leaders in Washington's public affairs gathered together to pay tribute to the Chief Justice and to dedicate him in the name of God to his important and responsible position in the judicial branch of our government.

Citizens of every political and religious faith must feel a sense of security in realizing that our President understands the importance of prayer and faith in God in the solution of our ills. It interested me very much to read the story about the criticism that came to President Eisenhower during the campaign for talking too much about religion. General Eisenhower refused to be swayed from his path. He said: "There is a great yearning and hunger among the people of this country for religion and I meet more and more people who are not ashamed to express it."

Then President Eisenhower, at his Inauguration, electrified the citizens of our beloved country by opening his address with a beautiful prayer.

Further, it was my privilege to attend another Prayer Breakfast a few months ago in our nation's capital. It was one of the most significant meetings ever held. The President of the United States, members of the Supreme Court, cabinet officers, members of Congress of both parties, business and professional leaders gathered together to renew their faith in God and in the efficacy of prayer. It was indeed comforting to hear the President stress that prayer was an absolute necessity. It is good to know that our leaders are relying upon God in the difficult days ahead.

The President, on that occasion, said:

Without a continuation of the basic principles on which our nation was founded, our system of government cannot endure. Only a people, strong in Godliness, is a people strong enough to overcome tyranny and make themselves free and others free. . . . You can't explain free government in any other terms than religious. The Founding Fathers had to refer to the Creator in order to make their revolutionary experiment make sense; it was because all men are endowed by their Creator with certain inalienable rights that men could dare to be free. They wrote their religious faith into our founding document, stamped their trust in God on the faces of their coins and currency and put it boldly at the base of our institutions. And when they drew up their bold Bill of Rights, where did they put Freedom of Worship? First, in the cornerstone position. That was no accident.

The paramount issue of the day is this: Do we still have religion in the cornerstone position in our hearts?

A crusade known as the March of Freedom is being led by Dr. Paul S. Reese, a prominent Minneapolis minister who recognizes the issue in this pronouncement:

"Because the forces of evil in the world are bent on destroying our religious freedom as guaranteed by the Constitution of the United States of America, and because these same forces of evil are bent on destroying the very foundations of our democracy whose Constitution owes its validity to the moral order of the universe and its future to a continuance of its popular form of government, and because America needs to be reminded of its great spiritual heritage and its responsibility to Almighty God as its sovereign ruler," it is proposed that on each July 4—our Independence Day—the President of the United States, the Vice President, Members of the Cabinet, Members of the Senate, Members of the House of Representatives, Justices of the Supreme Court, governors and state officials and all citizens reaffirm their faith in the seven freedoms portrayed in God's Holy Bible and specifically referred to in Psalm 23 as follows:

1. FREEDOM FROM WANT—"The Lord is my shepherd *I shall not want.*"

2. FREEDOM FROM HUNGER—"He maketh me to lie down in *green pastures.*"

3. FREEDOM FROM THIRST—"He leadeth me beside the *still waters.*"

4. FREEDOM FROM SIN—"He *restoreth* my soul and leadeth me in the paths of righteousness for His name's sake."

5. FREEDOM FROM FEAR—"Yea, though I walk through the valley of the shadow of death, I will *fear no evil:* for Thou art with me; Thy rod and Thy staff they comfort me."

6. FREEDOM FROM DANGER—"Thou preparest a table before me in the *presence of mine enemies.*"

7. FREEDOM TO LIVE ABUNDANTLY—"Thou anointest my head with oil; my cup runneth over. Surely goodness and mercy shall follow me all the days of my life: and I *will dwell in the house of the Lord for ever.*"

If on each Independence Day the same commitment is repeated, then that day will have the sacred significance it ought to have in the lives of our people.

This job of building a better country is not only for the President of the United States, it is a job for every individual citizen. It will be accomplished only by the acceptance of individual responsibility. Every citizen must understand the profound significance of freedom—not freedom only to have a good time, to exploit our natural resources for selfish purposes, to indulge in bigotry or prejudice, or to push other nations around. If that be our conception of freedom, then the holy light of freedom will soon be extinguished. If we are to keep freedom's Light from being extinguished, it must be kept holy!